PARADISE FOUND

Clarkson Potter Publishers
New York

PARADISE
FOUND
Gardening In
Unlikely Places

REBECCA COLE

Photographs By Helen Norman

Published by Clarkson Potter/Publishers,
201 East 50th Street, New York, New York
10022. Member of the Crown Publishing
Group.

Random House, Inc. New York, Toronto,
London, Sydney, Auckland
www.randomhouse.com

CLARKSON N. POTTER, POTTER, and
colophon are registered trademarks of
Random House, Inc.

Printed in China
Design by Laurie Wolfe

Library of Congress Cataloging-in-
Publication Data
Cole, Rebecca.
    Paradise found / by Rebecca Cole. — 1st ed.
    1. Gardens—Design. 2. Landscape gar-
dening. 3. Container gardening. 4. Garden
ornaments and furniture. I. Title.
SB473.C6424   2000
712'.6—dc21   99-24767
        CIP

ISBN 0-609-60415-5

10 9 8 7 6 5 4 3

FOR CURT, TIM AND JEFF . . .
THE BEST BROTHERS A GIRL COULD ASK FOR

ACKNOWLEDGMENTS

It was a hot, sunny morning at the tail end of August when I typed the last word to the last chapter of this book. To celebrate, I decided to mow my much-neglected lawn. Conquering the six-inch grass that hid countless forms of wildlife seemed a fitting end to a book on controlling nature by design.

Only the swath of grass under the overgrown viburnum hugging the side of the house remained, when it happened. I was swarmed by hundreds of angry bees that burrowed through the thick cotton of my sweatpants. I screamed and stripped naked on my front lawn, but it was too late. I was stung from head to toe. Nancy quickly led me inside the house to recuperate and rest, but ten minutes later I passed out. I stopped breathing and looked bad.

If it wasn't for Nancy Blaine and the men and women of the volunteer Sandwich Fire and Rescue Squad who rushed to my house that August morning, I would not be here today. From the bottom of my heart, I thank you for keeping me here a little longer.

As for the bees, I appreciate the lesson in the futility of trying to control nature. I got the message.

If there was one person who truly made this book possible, it would have to be Jessica Smith. She had her hand in every garden and her mind on every detail of the business. What would I ever do without her level head, sense of humor, and strong muscles?

And thanks go to the rest of the Potted Gardens staff who makes so many wonderful things grow: Gloria Sanchez, Rawle Dover, Julius "O'Neill" Williams, Arnoldo Iglesius, Panchita Guaderramma, and Maria Vlahos.

I'm grateful to my wonderful clients and friends who allowed us the privilege of working on and shooting in their private Edens: Luigi Caiola; Sean McGill and Luke, Sharon and Steve Kess; Sharon and Larry Morse;

Christy Turlington; Christine Burgin; Atlas and William Wegman; Mark Heithoff and Meredith Ross; Katherine Hufschmid and James Murdock; Pearl Gordon and Ed Corrigan; Del Bryant and Carolyn Smith-Bryant; Jim Gerity; Neale and Margaret Albert; Peter, Patrick, and Mark Elmore; Mary Emmerling; Patrick Dacy; and Gail Furman.

Thank you to Vito Masiello for finding the best old furniture a girl could wish for, and to David Kressler for always "holding the bag." Thanks to Cindy Gunn for her great pillows and to Maximo and Jose of M&J Iron Works for turning metal into art.

A very special thank you goes to my great brothers, Curtis, Tim, and Jeff, for their unflinching support of their favorite sister, and to the rest of my wonderful family for all their love and laughter, especially Dad and Martha Cole and Betty and Vincent Blaine.

Thank you to my agent, Charlotte Sheedy, who has taught me the meaning of living big. Thank you, too, for introducing me to Annetta Hanna, my editor, whose wise, encouraging, and patient nature shaped this book. I'm grateful to art director Marysarah Quinn whose thoughtful eye guided this book.

It is to my feisty artistic team that I am most indebted: my photographer, Helen Norman, whose eye, passion, and vision made all the gardens look good even out of bloom, and Laurie Wolfe, whose designs really made our work soar. Thanks to Carla Grande for leading them to me.

Thanks go to Shazi for keeping Chroma Zone open in the middle of the night, and to the wonderful crew at Bissett Nursery, headed by sweet Joey who never laughed when our trucks were too small and our plant selections too big; to Declan Keane and Estelle Irrigations for keeping the water flowing, and David Harrigel for casting some beautiful light on the subject; to Joe and Hillary at Fischer and Page for their constant teasing, endless flirting, and damn good flowers.

To my cousin Allison McNamara and her mom, Aunt Ruth Ann; Cara Palladino; Peggy Roeder; Carolyn and Lily Jun Patierno; Mo, Hank, Caitlin and Ross Offinger; Ryan Smith; Dori Smith; Sandy Seaman; Jody McNatt; Russel Pritchard; Timmy and Bob Nolan; David Skovron; Krim Boughalem; Lorie Baker; and Mary Alfano, thank you for being good friends, humorous critics, and great cooks—the essential ingredients to any good book. And to the O'Neil's, the Biggars, and Julie Fisher McKenna, . . . thanks for the memories.

CONT

ENTS

NDING
YOUR BLISS

"You have an old-fashioned sensibility, and you got it from growing up here," Nancy exclaims as we narrowly miss a buoy with the tip of the canoe. The summers my senses were coming alive I spent swimming, fishing, and boating on what looks today like a protected wilderness refuge. Yet tucked behind every other hundred-year-old pine tree is a camp (the New England word for summer lake house). Each home is painted either brown or green to match the dense forest that hugs the shore. On tiny islands, the old trees seem to droop and bend, as if attempting to get a second drink from above.

This year, submerged under twenty-six inches of spring rain, the docks and flooded banks leave an eerie calm. Paddling through the crystal-clear water of this beautiful lake, we feel like we have wandered into the nineteenth century or discovered a part of America not yet found.

Back in New York City, Mario informs me, "Modern's back," from the other end of the ten feet of farm table we are trying to fit into the tiniest store in New York City . . . mine. "Are you saying this table won't sell?" I ask him. "No, only that it won't stay in New York." I comfort my twinge of buyer's remorse with the fact that Potted Gardens is a garden and antique store, and thankfully garden lovers are old-fashioned types generally not subject to the whims of New York decorators. The farm table sold quickly, while my sixties porch furniture languished until Mario, out of pity, took it off my hands. His store, just down the

It was a grand childhood of summers spent in the Lake Region at the foot of the White Mountains, PREVIOUS and FOLLOWING PAGES. My early lessons in enjoying the great New Hampshire outdoors: tractor and wheelbarrows, dog training, and mountain climbing in matching outfits!

MY FIRST LESSONS IN

ENJOYING THE GREAT OUTDOORS

FAMILY VACATIONS ON "GOLDEN

POND" INSPIRE AN OLD-FASHIONED SOUL

street from mine, is full of whimsical and elegant reflections of modern, urban life. My sixties set was gone from there in three days!

It is out of necessity for a nourished soul that I divide my life between New Hampshire and New York City. I do not think I could live full-time in either place. In the dead of winter, I hibernate next to my woodstove, looking out at the White Mountains aptly covered with ten feet of white snow, and wonder if I should have waited one more year to redo the roof. In May I hold "high-level" business meetings at my favorite outdoor café a block from my New York showroom, dipping Tuscan bread in virgin olive oil, and wonder if I should have waited one more year to buy a large truck.

My garden designs are informed as much by my contemporary city life, as by my old-fashioned soul. But what I have learned over the years is that, as much as they would like to, none of my friends or clients have the time to garden the way our grandparents, or even our parents, did. Gardens that are easily maintained, not too tough to install, and livable are essential to today's lives. By and large, we have the time and space for only one garden and typically a small one at that. Gone are the days of the cutting garden, the children's garden, the vegetable garden, the perennial garden, and the strolling garden, each separately designed and maintained on one piece of property. Private and city-funded botanical gardens are the closest most of us will come to enjoying these theme gardens. Today we must get the most out of what little we have.

Sometimes that little—whether measured in terms of space or time—may seem completely inadequate. But for all those who think a garden paradise is out of reach, do not despair. It is possible to create your own

An eclectic mix of garden furniture, from old nineteenth-century iron benches to a little lady's chair slipcovered to sit on a covered porch in the summer, adorned Potted Gardens. ABOVE: Beautiful silk pillows with a photo-transfer of an old botanical painting from the turn of the century make the perfect accent to any garden room. RIGHT: The old iron fence from France, a coffee maker from a train in New England, a Victorian mirror from Virginia, and an egg basket from Pennsylvania work together quite nicely despite never having met before!

little Eden in the most unlikely places and with very few resources. The following pages reveal gardens, both modest and grand, that have emerged from problem spaces. Each new challenge has opened the door to some inventive solution. It is my belief that if you are willing to face the reality of the limitations upon your space, finances, abilities, and time, you can discover a creative interpretation of your own garden paradise.

As my gardens become larger and more elaborate, my designs become simpler. I have a recurring dream of awakening in a strange but familiar place. It is dark and quiet, not frightening but not at all clear. A door opens and I am nearly blinded for a minute as I adjust to the warm sunlight. I follow a stone path that leads to a large tree. Under the tree is a long wooden table with a chair on either end. I sit, rest my head on my arms atop the table, and wake. It is to this place of rest, this garden, I return. It is the essence of this peaceful resting spot I long to re-create. There are few flowers to speak of and no view; it is utter simplicity.

For the half of the year I spend in New York City, I have created a garden very much like my dream. It has few flowers; it is a place to rest; it is utterly peaceful. It reminds me of a narrow road in Sienna, Italy, one of my very favorite cities. The truth is it is just a back alley between two old townhouses, with very little sun and too many walls. But with a little imagination and a very strong will, I have created my own urban paradise.

To everyone's surprise, it is the other half of the year that I spend in the country that I have no garden, simple or otherwise. And it is not for lack of property: alas, I have my quaint little house in the Lake Region of New

PREVIOUS PAGES: Some of the old furniture ended up in the garden while most will accompany a modern sofa to create a "garden-style" room indoors. ABOVE: Lady's mantle and roses arranged in a tiny old urn can make a shady garden seem awash in sunshine. RIGHT: My own garden was conceived on a trip to Tuscany, long before I found this back alley in the middle of New York City.

WINDING PATHS
ALWAYS ADD MYSTERY TO A GARDEN

Hampshire with a couple of acres that could provide ample gardening opportunity. But since I began making a living gardening for others, I have found very little warm weather left at the end of planting season to plant and nurture a garden of my own. Not that I suffer from a lack of natural beauty. Rural paradise to me is a mountain view and a few wildflower seeds tossed around the covering to my well in the country. But I can't even provide pictures of this quasi-garden of mine for your entertainment: my brother Jeff recently mowed it down, thinking it was a patch of overgrown weeds. Ah well, it will return in a few weeks.

Although most of my design business is in New York City, the problems I encounter are common to small gardens everywhere. Each new garden and owner poses some unique challenges. The gardens in this book were all planted for busy people with awkward spaces but lots of desire to smell the roses. And so these pages reveal the myriad possible—and a few uncommon—garden problems.

FACING REALITY

The first step to any good garden design is to figure out what you want to do in your garden. When designing a garden for a client, I begin by asking them to picture themselves in their completed garden. Many envision themselves sleeping in a hammock, though some imagine their children playing among the flowers. The outdoorsy ones see themselves tanning in the sun, while the intellectual types are reading on a porch swing, and the writers are working at an old farm table under a canopy.

Before you draw a line or order a bush, decide how and where you want to enjoy your green space. Every garden should reflect the personality of its owner. If the most important element of your garden is that it provides visual delight from inside your house, then design your garden from your living room couch. Move from room to room and couch to chair to find all the best views of your potential garden. If you love to entertain and want garden parties every other weekend in the summer, keep this in

PREVIOUS PAGES: When I moved into the townhouse in the West Village, there was no garden. Three weeks later, after removing the brick path and 1950s white railing and adding large-river-stone flooring, 150-year-old terra-cotta balustrades, and 100 shady plants, I was giddy from overwork and ecstatic with the outcome. An exotic combination of bupleurum, lotus pods, and kale was tossed into a bucket to bring out the architecture for our inaugural garden party. LEFT: For completely low-maintenance planting, try rudbeckia for sunny areas in the ground. And try Marguerite daisies, ABOVE, for container gardening.

mind in your design: consider laying some kind of patio that would be good for dancing and plant only around the edges.

If you picture yourself curled up on a settee pretending to read while actually sleeping, you may want to start with some very comfortable seating. Since furniture can be as important to a garden as it is in the living room, choose solid, beautiful pieces that suit your needs. Plastic chairs and Plexiglas café tables will do little to enhance your flowers or the neighborhood aesthetic. Just as it's important to choose trees and perennials that will last for many years to come, choose furniture that you will not tire of by next season.

Some people do not see themselves resting in their garden at all. My father, for example, loves to work in his. He loves to work in my yard when he visits. He cannot sit still if there is a weed poking up, a branch out of place, or a hedge with little green shoots. It all must go, and it must go now. He is the ideal candidate for plants that require regular feeding, pruning, staking, attention of any kind. His garden in Florida has no seating, only lush, beautiful, ever-blooming flowers that need constant attention to keep from taking over the entire neighborhood.

KNOW WHAT YOU WANT

Despite the endless variety of personality types and garden types, we can identify a few basic preferences. There is, for example, the desire to have lots of blossoms all the time. And there are several ways to achieve this continual flowering in your garden. Using annuals exclusively means that a garden can continually bloom from spring to fall. One can achieve a little more complicated continual blooming schedule by planting perennials that bloom at different times. As the lilac and the spirea fade, the monarda blooms, and as that is ending the coreopsis begins and the

PREVIOUS PAGES, LEFT: The architectural elements and bouncy metal chair help keep this tiny garden interesting year round. RIGHT: The elegant addition of this curved staircase created an ideal stage for a collection of large to small pots of ivy that one day will cover the brick wall. Nearly all annuals need constant deadheading throughout the summer: Shasta daisies, TOP, and pansies, ABOVE, can bloom for four months if they are diligently cut back. RIGHT: Annuals and tender perennials are perfect for the underplanting of containers because they require little root space, which may be needed for a tree.

LOW-MAINTENANCE PLANTS EQUAL
LOTS OF **RELAXATION**

echinacea will follow. Some perennials are considered continual bloomers, but even they need constant feeding and pruning to keep showing off. Some varieties of roses will bloom for three months. To extend your blooming season even longer, you can plant bulbs in the fall to come up just as the snow is beginning to disappear in early spring.

Another basic gardening preference is for low maintenance, although there could not be a more relative term in all of gardening. For some, "low maintenance" means I never have to touch my garden. Unless plastic flowers will do, these people will need a water system *and* a full-time gardener.

For others, low maintenance means a profusion of constant blooms that need little more than watering care. Annuals are often considered low-maintenance plants. More accurately, they are easy to grow with constant maintenance. Most annuals will not perform well a few weeks following their initial planting unless they are deadheaded and fed regularly.

Still others consider a well-thought-out perennial garden to be low maintenance. To accomplish a symphony of different colors that reveals itself slowly over spring, summer, and fall, a perennial garden is, in fact, needed.

Low maintenance, constant blooms, lots of color: one of these may be your top priority. But it is important that you do not begin and end with your number-one priority. For instance, if color is your priority but your flowering perennial or annual garden does not include ground covers or evergreens, there will be nothing to look at once your colorful blooms die back. Alas, a colorful garden with no structure can be as bland as a piece of raisin toast without butter.

Begin your design by listing all your dreams for your garden and then see if one precludes another. Most of my clients think they have one goal in mind for their garden. They'll say, for instance, "I want an English country-style garden," or "I want to be able to enjoy my garden from the bedroom." The

PREVIOUS PAGES: Low-maintenance plants by no means result in no color. The snowmound spirea, LEFT, blooms for weeks in May, giving way to the pinks of monarda in early summer, RIGHT, on this rooftop eighteen stories up in New York City. ABOVE: Variegated ivies need more sun than the solid green varieties, but there are dozens to choose from in each category to hold plenty of interest for years. RIGHT: In this townhouse's partly shady backyard, wisteria covers the neighboring wall, while birch trees dot the multileveled seating areas. Every ray of sunshine works to nourish the echinacea that thrive near an oakleaf hydrangea.

most common gardening goals I hear are: low maintenance, lots of flowers all the time, lots of green in the winter, an open view, lots of privacy, and enough room for a table with six chairs. Often this list comes from one person!

When your wish list is completed, circle your two top priorities. If these are in conflict, like low maintenance *and* lots of flowers all the time, one has got to give. You can certainly have some elements from each but not all of both. But before eliminating flowers altogether because they seem like too much work, try some easy-to-maintain plants to find out what kind of gardening tasks you enjoy. You may be surprised by how much fun gardening work can be. Most people who want to look at a garden will enjoy puttering in it if someone tells them how. It is the fear of the unknown that keeps most of us from venturing into new territory. Start small, introduce new plant varieties slowly, and ask lots of questions of wise gardeners about their care.

Another tricky combination of wishes is to have lots of flowers and green all winter. If you have a large space, you can pick areas that would best accomplish each of these goals. If your space is limited, however, you may have to weigh the importance of each and set priorities. I find that when most people say they want green year-round, what they really mean is that they want something attractive to look at in the winter. Evergreen shrubs and trees are nice in large spaces, but they can be rather overpowering in small flowering areas. Airier deciduous trees can make a better flower companion, and they offer plenty of interest in the winter even without their leaves.

In container gardens, when underplanting with annuals, mix in English ivy to provide just enough green in the winter months. I like to use woody shrubs with serpentine branches that flower and produce berries, like spirea or cotoneaster, instead of solid evergreens. Their woody stems provide lovely architectural structure in

LEFT: Ivy and myrtle topiaries can thrive for years in diffused light. They need regular pruning of new growth to keep their shape and regular watering to assure that enough water reaches up their long stems to their new leaves. RIGHT: The shiny, waxy architectural leaves of hollies and the gritty, dull finish of old stone statuary make a striking combination of textures.

the winter months even after the leaves drop off. If you are lucky enough to have snow on them, all the better.

If your wish list includes low maintenance *and* green all winter, you are in luck. A garden need not be all living and green. I adore a garden of statues or architectural elements covered with ivy. It's classic, simple, and low maintenance. Steer away from larger evergreens in a container garden. They tend to overpower most pots. If you are gardening in the ground and want to block a view or wall, you have a wide range of terrific evergreen choices. Some of my personal favorites are Japanese junipers, holly, and Leyland cypress.

The need for low maintenance *and* the desire to just sleep, read, and eat in your garden could potentially be in conflict. I would suggest beginning with the comfortable furniture and then working a simple garden around it. An irrigation system is essential to this plan if you're gardening in containers. Without it, watering during the summer months could take more than an hour a day.

THOUGHTS ON PAPER

Once you have established your priorities and your garden's purpose, go out onto your terrace or into your yard and just sit. Gaze around, find your natural lookout spot, close your eyes, and imagine how your garden might look. Don't worry about *how* this will be accomplished. Do not bring out any gardening books yet. Just sit and dream.

If absolutely nothing comes, hire someone.

For everyone else, get a piece of paper and draw an aerial view of your whole yard or terrace. Indicate the permanent elements: the house, big trees, the driveway, a walkway, a skylight, a vent, and so on. Then choose the major focal points in your garden. Usually these areas are already chosen for you; they can be the corners of your patio, the fence off to the outer edge of your

Temperament may be the most important element in designing your garden. If your dream is to sit in the shade, relax and read, ABOVE, create a small container garden on a porch with large comfy furniture. If playing is the goal, RIGHT, consider a rope swing hanging from an industrial fence; sturdy ivy can withstand some trapeze practice.

yard, the large oak tree in the middle of your lawn, the skylights off to the right of your roof deck. Whatever structure or point draws your eye naturally is often the best place to begin your garden design—unless, of course, your eye is drawn to an ugly spot. If so, choose a brand-new focal area that will draw attention away from the eyesore. Once the primary areas are selected, two or three secondary ones should be chosen for balance. For instance, if some planting is to be done in front of a fence to the east, consider an area off to the west to complement and balance it.

You will need to determine just how much light each of these areas receives. Observe them over the course of a few days. Keep in mind that in the same small space, microclimates will occur. One side of your terrace may get sun all day, while the other corner loses light by late morning because of a neighboring building. To add to the confusion, remember that the sun shifts throughout the year. An area that may be in full sun in the early spring could be in full shade by late fall. Most plants that require sun need it most in the spring and early summer. If you get seven or more hours of sun a day, your garden could be considered to have "full sun." Since, excluding winter, there is an average of fourteen hours of sun on any given day in the summer, anything short of seven hours will range from full to partial shade.

THE BONES

Once you have a rough sketch of where and how big your garden areas will be, and you know their sun conditions, you can begin to select the plants. Begin with the "bones" of your garden. These are your large plants, the

Learn to love the industrial elements of your space. The fire escape stairs, LEFT, add the drama and "bones" necessary to anchor this urban oasis on a rooftop, smack in the middle of downtown. The rusty smokestack, RIGHT, next to the lime-colored new leaves serves as the perfect trellis for a climbing wisteria.

trees or big shrubs. The bones can also be architectural elements like fencing or statuary. In each of your garden areas you will need some large elements.

I like to begin my shopping list with trees. When counting how many will go in your garden, keep in mind trees grow . . . and grow . . . and grow. If you are planting trees in containers, I recommend Jacquemontii birch, styrax, Japanese maple, Japanese juniper, and Leyland cypress. I have found these to be among the best container performers. To the disappointment of most of my clients, the styrax is the only bloomer in my group of favorites. Over the years of planting fruit trees in pots, I have not been impressed with their performance. Unless they are fed constantly, they tend to grow straight up and produce little to no fruit. And even with constant feeding, not much fruit will appear until the second or third year. Finally, keep in mind that if you feed a tree in a container constantly, it will likely outgrow that container much sooner than you may wish to transplant it.

If you do have some room and if there are very few trees on your property, consider planting the giants: oak, elm, maple. Place the trees a good distance from any areas where you envision lots of flowers blooming. Big trees will surely block the sun. Shade gardens can be elegant, interesting, and green, whereas sunny gardens will bloom and show much more color. And though I think blooms are overrated, most people cannot live without lots of them. For gardens planted in the ground, fruit trees and flowering shrubs, such as lilac and hydrangeas, make wonderfully blooming "bones" that do not obstruct much sun from smaller perennials.

When a small garden is surrounded by walls, the only thing to do is to garden up! ABOVE: Porcelain vine will not attach itself to a wall; it needs something to wind itself around, like a beautiful old fence simply leaning against a wall. RIGHT: Scaevola and geraniums fill this highrise ledge, securely fastened with wires wrapped around the pot and railing.

Once you have chosen these large elements, map out the areas immediately surrounding them. Keep in mind that nature is not rigid. Unless you want a very formal garden, there's no need to make perfect circles or squares in front of your lilac bush or picket fence. Let your garden meander around the focal points and the larger elements. Do not make your three main garden areas all the same size. Expand into the center of your property, then come in only partway on the sides for a natural balance.

Once the larger architectural items are positioned, begin arranging the furniture, on paper. Consider nestling a table and chair right up to your garden areas. If it looks like your seating is too spread out, extend your planting into the center or add another garden area off center. Create some intimacy and interest by breaking up a large space with different sets of furniture.

Once you have a rough idea of your garden on paper, return to the yard or terrace and mark off the spots that will hold plants and furniture. If you are anything like me, this is the first of many times you will make adjustments. If you are a visual person, use real chairs and some actual plants to mark off your areas. For the more analytical types, a drawing to scale may suffice.

Once you have a very rough idea of the key elements of your garden, it is time to consider the details: which tree should be planted in that shady spot? Should the table be round or square? Should the containers be iron or wood? It is in these decisions that a patch of green becomes a garden of one's own. Look for inspiration in catalogs, nurseries, books, and neighbors' gardens. Draw elements from each and put together an altogether unique slice of paradise.

Industrial L-brackets and galvanized fencing can be most appropriate for an urban environment, LEFT, while a stone wall can serve as the ideal "bones" for a rural setting, ABOVE.

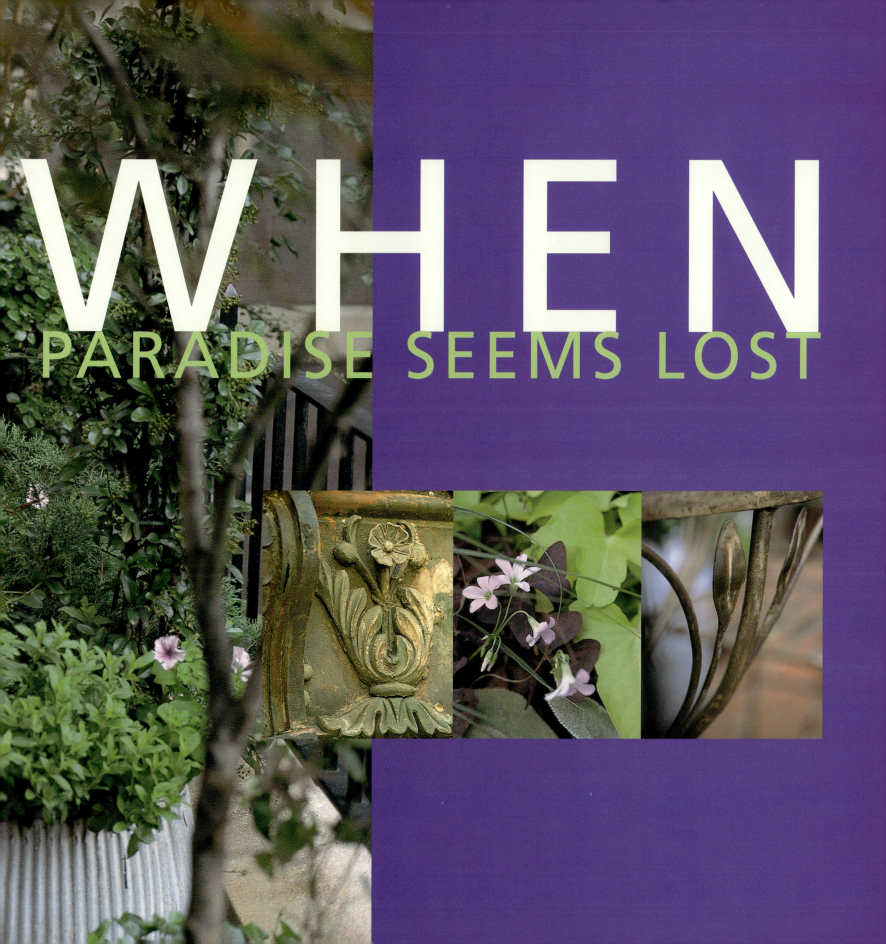

WHEN
PARADISE SEEMS LOST

THE TINY TERRACE

The typical terrace in New York City measures about forty square feet. These tiny outdoor spaces are coveted squares that can increase the market value of an apartment by more than 50 percent. When looking at these tiny cement plots, it is difficult to imagine that they can become urban oases. Thankfully, imagination is not as limited as space.

I met Megan ten days after she moved to New York from San Diego. Megan is the kind of person you wish there were more of in New York: kind and energetic, she has lots of friends in lots of places. She wanted a garden in New York to entertain and relax in, but she was not a descendant of the Rockefellers. After an exhausting search, she had found a small one-bedroom apartment with a tiny terrace that she could afford. The only draw-back was that it was a sixth-floor walk-up. She enthusiastically asked me to help her with her garden, and I laid out one stipulation: she would have to hire Olympic athletes to haul the twenty-five containers, fifty assorted items of plant material (including trees), and fifty thirty-quart bags of soil up her six flights of stairs.

This tiny terrace has become Megan's urban oasis, full of pansies, salvia, lavender, and ivy, ABOVE, while an old linen beach chair keeps her from longing for those summers at the shore, RIGHT.

GARDEN CHORES

CAN BE A LABOR OF LOVE

Megan agreed, and contracted with her moving company to haul the garden to the terrace. Meanwhile, we raced around collecting and buying containers, plants, trees, and soil in order to meet the movers, who would be arriving three days later with Megan's furniture from the West Coast. The foreman had not forewarned his poor crew of the arrangement, however, so when they saw us unloading our two small trucks, I thought there might be a walkout. Fortunately, one of the movers was a gardener from Ireland and another had spent his childhood on a farm in Honduras. Fueled by memories of roses grown in Kerry and strawberries near the equator, these two men made it possible for Megan to start creating some green memories of her own.

With the priority being simply to meet the movers, we had no time to formally design the garden. Of course, I rarely formally design any garden, but this time the sketch was hastily drawn on a cocktail napkin. We were really in a hurry.

Though the space was tiny, I thought it needed three trees to form the bones of the garden. Megan wanted a blooming tree and an evergreen. I wanted my usual favorite, all birches. A variety of trees can end up looking too busy in small spaces. Having uniformity in the larger pieces can actually expand the look of a tiny space. Fruit trees and other bloomers also need to have plenty of earth beneath their feet to start filling out like respectable trees. Due to our severely limited space, we could not provide a little cherry tree with a large enough container for it to grow out properly. The compromise

Amazingly, this tiny garden, surrounded by a country-style wooden fence for some privacy from the high-rise building nearby, also holds two clump river birch trees and one Japanese juniper. Rather than feeling too crowded in Manhattan, Megan now feels cozy, protected, and calm!

Megan and I made was to choose two fifteen-gallon Jacquemontii birch trees in two eighteen-inch square cedar boxes and one five-foot Japanese juniper in an eighteen-inch round terra-cotta pot.

Remember: when choosing plants, keep in mind the primary purpose for your garden. For Megan, her garden was to serve as a refuge from a high-stress corporate job. I believed that the best ways to accomplish this were to provide her with a wonderful view of a cozy English-style garden from her bedroom and to give her simple gardening tasks that she could do daily to help unwind. When space is limited, most container gardens will benefit tremendously from a profusion of annuals underplanted around every perennial plant. These bedding plants do need to be deadheaded constantly, and that was just the kind of easy task Megan could use to relax after a long day.

The hard edges of her rectangular terrace would have to be altered to achieve an English country-garden feel. A common mistake in terrace gardening is to follow the straight lines of the outer edges with rectangular or square planters. Use round containers instead or angle square ones on the diagonal in the corners; this allows your rigid straight edges to soften. Megan's all but disappeared once we added squiggly, flowing shrubs and vines such as spireas (in place of the typical boxwood), cotoneasters, and climbing hydrangeas.

Once everything made it to the rooftop, the fun could begin. It is almost impossible to work when the space that is to be planted is completely filled up, so organization is essential. Jessica, gardener extraordinaire and on staff at Potted Gardens, prepared the pots. She drilled and pounded holes in all the containers so they would drain properly. She lined the wooden and metal boxes with industrial-strength garbage bags to prevent interior erosion and rust. Holes were punctured in the garbage bags directly over the hole in the container. A terra-cotta shard was placed into the hole in the plastic and in the hole in the container. Then Jessica filled all the containers halfway with soil.

Though Megan's garden is packed full of plants, the tight palette of the white and blue of pansies, ABOVE, and the silvers and blues of artemisia and lobelia, RIGHT, keeps the garden from becoming cluttered. Too much variety in color can look quite messy in a small space.

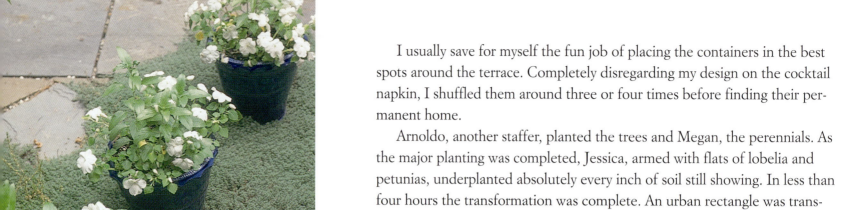

I usually save for myself the fun job of placing the containers in the best spots around the terrace. Completely disregarding my design on the cocktail napkin, I shuffled them around three or four times before finding their permanent home.

Arnoldo, another staffer, planted the trees and Megan, the perennials. As the major planting was completed, Jessica, armed with flats of lobelia and petunias, underplanted absolutely every inch of soil still showing. In less than four hours the transformation was complete. An urban rectangle was transformed into Megan's oasis. She was no longer homesick for San Diego.

The next day we were all invited to a cocktail party to inaugurate her garden. More than thirty people came to admire Megan's little Eden. Because of the terrace's small size, no more that eight or so guests could fit outside at one time, but a lively debate ensued as to whether the garden had existed before she moved in. No one could believe it had arrived the day before: our "before" pictures seemed to settle the debate but not the surprise!

HALF SHADE, HALF SUN

Nestled behind the brownstones of an unassuming block on the Upper East Side of Manhattan is one of my favorite gardens. It belongs to a television news producer who is seldom home. He wanted a garden that required very little maintenance but would hold his and his friend's interest as they unwound from traveling the world.

The yard was oddly shaped, with a long, dark, narrow walkway just outside the back door that suddenly opens onto a big, bright patio area. We both loved the existing brick flooring that took up half the space, although we had little attachment to the old gray slate that filled the other half. Because of time and money constraints, we decided to keep all the old flooring and plant woolly thyme around the edges of the brick and the slate, tying the two mismatched surfaces together. We also let some weeds grow through the loose separations between bricks to give the feeling that this patio had been here for centuries.

The smokestacks along the outer walls held some allure for both of us, so we planted wisteria to wrap itself around the vents without fully covering them. We were happy to leave the large hydrangea, which was clearly decades old, well enough alone. English ivy had completely taken over the cement walls surrounding the garden. We hacked and yanked out chunks of it to make way for brighter nooks and crannies of white impatiens, and to create some architectural interest. An old wire screen covers one wall, and ivy magically flourishes on each side of it. Little mossy terra-cotta pots, old painted sap buckets, royal blue glazed pots, and stone corbels all add detailed touches that gave this garden its depth. Along the dark path where precious little grows, we placed Greek olive urns; nothing more is needed.

The furniture is simple, old, and untouched. It looks like it has been in this garden forever. Cracking paint matches the old walls. All is in peaceful harmony.

PREVIOUS PAGES: The old-fashioned look of hydrangeas is perfectly complemented by the old-fashioned French bistro table and chairs. Even the blue and white of the old chipping paint matches the blue and white of the blossoms! LEFT and ABOVE: The repetition of similar elements can tie any garden together nicely.

A WEED IS SIMPLY A FLOWER

LOOKING FOR A GOOD HOME

A LONG AND NARROW TERRACE

A few years ago I was asked to look at some plans a nursery had drawn up for a new terrace garden. It was a very difficult space in which to work: forty feet long and only five feet wide. It was visible from the dining room, the kitchen, the library, and the office. The owners were doctors who wanted to use the garden to relax, eat breakfast, and read the paper. They had cut out pictures of gardens in Tuscany with trellises and narrow paths, but they feared their existing design conveyed none of this feeling.

The owners' garden wish list included plenty of seating for relaxing and eating, a meandering path, a trellis, low maintenance, and the feeling of a protective, cozy haven. The nursery's plan only accentuated the long narrowness of the space. We needed to cozy it up by breaking it into a few separate areas. So, we concentrated on the views from each room. A simple pergola made of plumber's piping would surround the kitchen window. The office at the far end of the terrace had an ugly wall as its view, so we decided to hide it with a couple of five-foot Leyland cypress trees. At the other end of the terrace was the library, where a meandering path through the entire length of the garden could be seen. We would highlight the view from the dining room with a beautiful Japanese maple.

The color scheme was drawn from Tuscany: terra-cotta, rusty oranges, and deep greens. Since there were no ready-made containers that could both

PREVIOUS PAGES: The old brick patio was our inspiration for this "Tuscan" garden where the shadiest spot is lined with olive jars because little will grow there. LEFT: Maria trains ivy up an iron pergola that was added halfway down a forty-foot-long terrace to create some much-needed intimacy and coziness. ABOVE: It was easy finding rusty old tins to match the rust-and-green color scheme.

fit the narrow terrace and provide enough space for the trees we wanted, we built four large containers. The pergola was also custom-made. I drew up simple plans for the containers and provided the metalworker with a sample of the color we wanted. We had to consider the weight of the boxes, since too much weight on a terrace is always a concern. And although we did have an elevator to work with this time, we would have to maneuver the boxes quite a distance to get them into place. We ended up choosing the thinnest sheet metal that could possibly hold up over fifteen years of outdoor use, approximately an eighth of an inch thick, with the corners both welded and bolted together. I wanted the bolts and the L-brackets to appear on the outside of the boxes rather than the inside, as my welder suggested, since I thought this added an industrial detail appropriate for an urban garden. We raised the boxes two inches off the ground on simple metal legs and drilled four half-inch holes into the bottoms for drainage. We were all thrilled with the results.

Two weeks after we had completed the garden, however, we received a call from one of the owners saying that the containers were rusting terribly. To arrest oxidation, our welder had put a couple of coats of rustproofing over the partially rusted metal, but she may not have applied enough coats. We wiped off the new rust and added three more coats of polyurethene sealer. Each year since, we have added two more coats. So far, the metal is holding the desired color and rusting no further.

Once the pergola was designed, it was apparent that we needed some rust-colored furniture to complement it. In a small space, it is as important to choose a limited color palette with the furniture as it is with the plants. We chose a beautiful steel table with a glass top and two elegant steel chairs. They were a shiny steel color that clashed with our rusty theme, so we scraped off the rustproofing finish and left them outside in the rain for two

Figs look more like art than breakfast on a new rust-patina glass tabletop, ABOVE, while an oakleaf hydrangea stands out among the greenery of a deeply shaded garden, LEFT.

weeks. Once they reached the desired shade of rust, we applied a coat of polyurethene that matched the pergola and the boxes.

My friends Steve and Marcello, from The Lively Set, found two matching old metal benches at a hospital auction in Ohio. They were painted green, and we went back and forth on whether to strip them to match the rest of the metal furniture. I usually err on the leave-well-enough-alone side, and since these were already painted green, the garden's neutral color, I won.

We experimented early on in this garden with some sun-loving perennials, such as echinacea and rudbeckia and lavender. I had hoped that the reflected sun from the windows of the buildings across the way might be enough to nourish some sun-loving blossoms. Alas, I was wrong. We had a deep-shade garden to contend with so we added some Japanese tassel fern, a spectacular oakleaf hydrangea, and lots of *Chaenomeles japonica.* To help his petunias along, Ed gave them weekly doses of bloom booster and a prayer, and we moved the Japanese maple to the sunniest spot on the terrace after its leaves started turning gray. Oxalis, bleeding hearts, ginger, and epimedium replaced the echinacea. English ivy and ajuga thrive at the edges of each container. The story of this garden is less about blooms and more about comfort, calm, and green.

The doctors tell me they meander along their narrow path each morning to the middle of the garden to read the paper and savor a cup of coffee. The two green hospital park benches hug the building walls and provide a sense of intimacy within the overcrowded landscape of the city just beyond the railing. Climbing roses and wisteria are just beginning to cover the pergola, but the two doctors are no longer in a hurry to complete their garden. They say they do not mind waiting a year or two for the covering to be full.

ABOVE: Some of the old 1930s iron hotel furniture is being remade with elegant and simple lines. A polyurethene finish that keeps water out halts oxidation before it destroys the metal. RIGHT: What once was a long strip of concrete with an iron rail becomes an urban paradise, complete with a winding path, two park benches, and a breakfast nook.

MIXING THE **NEW** WITH THE OLD IN PERFECT HARMONY

THE BACKYARD TOWNHOUSE

Jonathan and Priscilla are very busy people. He runs a newspaper and she is a financier. Both love old houses and modern conveniences. Old molding and modern furniture fill their townhouse in New York. The gas stove is an industrial relic from the twenties, refurbished to outdo the best appliances of the nineties. Their tiny backyard measures twenty feet wide by fourteen feet deep. Two sets of stairs, leading from the second and basement floors, break up this small space even further. The surrounding buildings wall in the garden on all four sides and up four stories. Turning this dark little cement plot into a garden was quite a challenge.

Priscilla and Jonathan have opposite tastes. He loves shiny new colorful pieces and she would be happy with a chunk of the Parthenon to accent their garden. Our goal, therefore, was to meld their differences into an exciting creative synthesis.

We approached the garden in stages. The first issue to solve was how to prevent the fifty-foot walls from dwarfing and darkening the already tiny space. A trellis was affixed to the back wall, and gallons of creamy yellow paint made a world of difference. Light now bounced all around the walls and made the space look much larger.

The next issue was the flooring. Since the garden was to be used largely for entertaining, we wanted to cover most of the area with a hard flooring surrounded by just enough soil for a few trees and some ground cover. A favorite flooring surface of mine is river stones, more commonly used for stone walls. Each stone is a completely different size; most of them are somewhat flat on at least one side, but they do vary tremendously in height and length, offering quite a challenge for who-

PREVIOUS PAGES: The old iron balcony railing from the kitchen above and the stone lion fountain on the far trellised wall, LEFT, frame this tiny townhouse garden. Each element was carefully chosen to either add color, as in the blue-tiled table and celadon green chairs, or hide wiring, as in the trellising and the tin ceiling tiles, RIGHT, filled with ivy and hanging from the side wall. ABOVE and FOLLOWING PAGES: Once the chairs were chosen, matching their lime green with the wonderful leaves of a scented geranium added the real punch we were looking for.

ever is laying them out. For a very natural look, it is best not to set them in cement but to use instead a soil and pebble mix as mortar. This way moss, creeping thyme, and ajuga can roam freely around the edges of each stone.

Once the floor and the walls were done, we felt we finally had something to work with. It was now time to think about the details of the garden and what plants we might like. Priscilla's wonderful collection of old architectural elements was to be the cornerstone of the garden design. A concrete lion's head was turned into a fountain simply by drilling a hole in his mouth and inserting a tube attached to a recirculating pump set into a tub of water. Originally we planned to erect three stone steps directly under the lion's-head fountain and rest a galvanized tub, filled with water, on the top step. Jonathan, who wanted some bold colors in the garden, had a better plan. He found a large ceramic pot with a royal blue glaze to add just the punch the garden needed. Miraculously, several days later Jonathan also found a spectacular tiled table in lime green and the same royal blue. Matching lime green French-styled bistro chairs came next, and the color scheme was complete.

Tying the color of the furniture to the color of the plants was the next step; that incredible lime green became my obsession. Leaves of nasturtiums, variegated lantana, and scented geraniums were perfect matches. The deep green of English ivy made the celadon green even more vibrant. What was once a hole was fast becoming a little Eden.

The overpowering height of the surrounding walls was still an issue. Luckily, my pack-rat self had salvaged chunks of a tin facade from a building being demolished a few years ago on the Lower East Side. We dug these pieces out of storage and hung them twelve feet up on one wall. This gives the illusion that the wall is a more appropriate twelve feet high, because your eye is drawn to the tin rather than the remaining thirty-five feet above it. The architectural facade also helped cover up some pipes and wires that the city owned and would not remove. To balance the garden, an old iron gate was placed along the opposite wall.

The rest of the garden design fell into place once these problems were solved. With a tiny garden it is difficult to achieve any real depth with plant material. We quickly were able to create variety and interest in Priscilla and Jonathan's backyard by using the architectural elements. We then edged the

SHADE IS MERELY A CHANCE FOR BOLD LEAVES AND COLORFUL FURNITURE TO SHOW OFF

LAYING
A RIVER-STONE F

Before any garden floor can be laid, drains must be installed. Then dig down about 8 inches below ground level. Pour 3 inches of pebbles or loose crushed concrete over the entire area. Slope evenly leveled ground away from the house and toward the drains.

1. Mix pebbles and soil together to use as mortar between the river stones.

2. Place rocks with smoothest side up in a puzzle pattern.

3. Dig down or add the soil-and-pebble mix as needed to level each stone.

4. Make sure the space between stones is about one inch all the way around.

5. Pack the soil mix down well and evenly around the edges of each rock.

6. Stomp on all the edges to test for looseness. The stones should not move. Add more soil and pebble mix as needed.

7. Clean off excess soil.

8. Plant moss, creeping thyme, or ajuga in the soil-and-pebble mix.

4

7

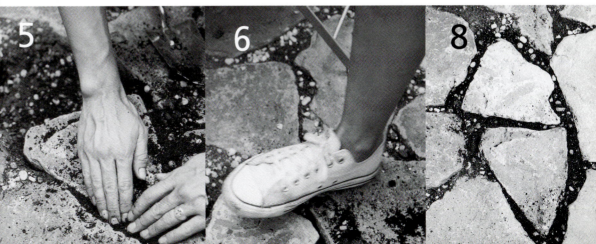

5

6

8

stone patio with trees planted in the ground, and used containers to create levels. A traditional perennial bed planted in the ground would have taken years and much more space to accomplish a similar look. Two clump birch trees covered the two far corners. One whole wall was edged with bamboo, which took off like crazy. The trees were all underplanted with ivy and ajuga, and flats of annuals were placed in pots.

TOO MUCH ROOM

When my cousin Mo bought a house a couple of miles from mine in New Hampshire, she asked if I would help with the landscaping. Hers was the opposite problem from that of my city clients: she had too much space. Those who live in the country or suburbs often have so much space that they can get overwhelmed simply trying to decide where to start. A big space is enough to push even the mildest of procrastinators into ten years of "When I have time to garden . . ."

First off, if extraordinary natural beauty surrounds you, buy a few great chairs and call it a day. It is difficult to do any better than Mother Nature.

But if you really want flowers, yet are overwhelmed by the grandeur of the land around you, start small. Start really small. Plant one spectacular container with a fantastic mix of annuals and place it in front of a gate or door. I guarantee that within days, that container will inspire some perennial planting nestled close by. Before long, an entire garden could sprout up almost without a plan!

Remember, masses of the same plants make a much more powerful effect than bits and pieces of dozens of different varieties. Do not skimp at the nursery. If you like delphinium, do not buy two plants; buy twenty.

ABOVE: A carpet of green grass and two large Adirondack chairs under a large oak tree are as American and delicious as apple pie. Don't mess with a good thing! Add a little birdhouse, RIGHT, if you feel the need to do something.

LARGE TREES ARE THE ANSWER TO

LARGE OPEN SPACES

When you fall in love with twenty different kinds of perennials, force yourself to narrow your choices, and buy only your favorite three. Make sure they work well together and buy lots of each, but do not buy them in equal quantities. Once you've placed the plants, fill in the holes with the secondary choices that will complement them.

When the eye can see vast distances around the area that is to become a garden, create focus with large trees or some bold architectural elements. Fences can make not only good neighbors but excellent garden companions as well. Stone walls, steps, birdbaths, and pools are also good elements with which to anchor a garden. If you already have any of these architectural pieces in place, great—begin your garden there. But if not, you may not know just where to position them. In that case, look around your space for a natural sitting area and place your elements there. Perhaps the crest of a little hill or an area facing the oldest tree on your property could be a start.

A fence will provide your garden with an instant background. If the fence is high, your plantings should be high also. Choose fencing that is appealing on its own. Good planting choices will help an ugly wall but will never hide it. Old wooden fencing, with great old paint and a bit of moss and lichen already attached, is one of my personal favorites. A stone wall winding around a crooked path just before veering into a wooded forest is like poetry to me. If you are not fortunate enough to have a stone wall surrounding your property, try to suggest that feeling when choosing a fence. Any natural-looking fence or wall is guaranteed to evoke instant charm.

LEFT: A wooden fence, a stone wall, and a magnificent old urn elegantly balance the large open space on the far side of the pool. ABOVE: An old Indonesian shutter with layers of paint complements perfectly the red monarda, purple echinacea, and pink achillea.

BEGINNERS LUCK OR IS THERE A

GENIUS AMONG US?

SVENGALI GARDENS

Shortly after I opened my shop, Mark became a regular visitor. Every couple of weeks an old bucket or a miniature rose would catch his eye and he would take it home. By his own admission he knew nothing about plants, but his curiosity and desire to learn warmed all who worked at Potted Gardens. He asked a million questions about the care of every plant he purchased. I once walked in on Gloria as she was explaining to him exactly how much water to put in the watering can, and how often and what time of day to do the deed. Each time he left, bets were placed on the number of days that particular plant purchase would survive.

The day my first book (*Potted Gardens*) arrived in my shop, Mark bought a copy. A week later he came in looking for larger outdoor containers rather than his usual small indoor variety. We never told our adorable young man how little confidence we had in his ability to make a garden on his rooftop. After all, the single women working at the store had decided they were happy with his increasingly regular visits and wanted to do nothing to discourage them.

We thought it best not to ask, and Mark did not volunteer any information about his garden's progress. Privately, we thought it must not be going well or he would surely have brought it up himself—so best not to pry.

In October of that year, Mark came into the shop and announced that he had completed his garden and was afraid he had done some things wrong. He said he did not know the names of most of the plants he'd used and he was not sure if the garden would survive the winter. He asked if I would walk through it with him to explain plant by plant what to do to protect it.

Given his irresistible enthusiasm, I obliged. It pains me to admit that I pictured a crude placement of a few plants and odd containers in a row, wilting under too little water on a hot, black tar roof. Why I had so little faith I am not sure. Maybe because there was so little ego involved when Mark asked the simplest gardening questions. Never did he boast about his progress; instead, he always emphasized how little he knew. He stressed that this was his first foray into gardening. He was a modest beginner.

My ego, on the other hand, is much more apparent, so it is hard to admit all this. When oxygen had finally returned to my lungs, a good seven minutes

PREVIOUS PAGES: This tour de force of line, scale, and plant variety is Mark's first try at gardening. Note his splendid use of grasses and ornamental trees. Mark and Meredith can relax under their Japanese maple, LEFT, thanks in part to their newly installed automatic watering system, ABOVE, since the water tower next door is little help to the always-thirsty thunbergia.

ROSES, RUST, AND BLACK TAR: ALL

ELEMENTS OF AN URBAN PARADISE...

after I'd climbed the four flights of long, steep stairs to his roof, I gasped for a new reason. Mark's urban garden was the best I had ever seen, better than any of my own. The levels, the containers, the choice of plants, the pergola . . . everything was magnificent! I grilled him: are you sure you have never gardened before? Do you have a degree in architecture or design? Did you hire someone to help you? Do you live with your mother or girlfriend, who designs terrace gardens for a living?

He complimented me by replying, "I read your book." I was flattered, disbelieving, and amazed. We began going through the garden inch by inch, but more for me than him.

He had built platforms from pressure-treated cedar first. He had constructed levels out of necessity, because the roof slanted so much. The result was that intimacy and interest were added.

Mark told me about a huge scrap-metal yard in Brooklyn that he would dig through for hours with no help or supervision. He would get the strongest-looking man there to chop up and haul out segments of reincarnated industrial garbage, which he would then turn into planters on his roof. He thought it best not to tell the guy what would become of these pieces, since it was more than likely the muscleman thought he was crazy already. I prayed he was not as observant about us.

The design of his pergola came from the water tower atop the building across the way. Mark repeated the metal L-bars with the same crisscross design as on the base of the water tower. Only a true artist could appreciate and copy the simple beauty and elegance of this practical industrial design. Mark was a true artist.

The design of the top of the pergola did not come as easily as the sides. He said he struggled with ideas and materials until a friend told him about the cable and pulleys used in small cranes. By simply drilling holes in the L-brackets and threading heavy cable through a pulley, Mark created a perfect home for city-dwelling wisteria. One more year and the wisteria would provide

PREVIOUS PAGES: Instead of covering up the black tar on the building's walls with lattice, it serves as a dramatic backdrop for English ivy and a 'New Dawn' rose. LEFT: This Rocky Mountain boy finally feels at home atop his city rooftop now that there is green. ABOVE: In the first year Mark built his simple, elegant, and industrial trellis, the wisteria already began to creep over the edges to cover the top.

ample shade from the scorching summer heat on this roof in lower Manhattan.

I learned so much that day, mostly about myself and my assumptions. I also met Mark's girlfriend, much to the dismay of the single gals back at the store. The grass patch he had planted on the slanted roof over the door is a bit of genius I know I will steal. And though I have been saying for years that you do not need any deep knowledge of horticulture to create a magnificent garden, I am not sure I actually believed it until that day. Mark is my inspiration.

THE FRONT PORCH

It was 1963. I was five. We lived on a tree-lined, dead-end street in Cincinnati, Ohio. I had two brothers, and we were close enough in age that we were often mistaken for triplets. The brick houses in our neighborhood were spaced evenly apart, each a little different, pulled together as much by camaraderie as by the sidewalk.

It was July 23 and ninety-five degrees before the sun was fully up, but our tiny front porch was ready. At least thirty people had gathered by eight A.M. We would have to wait at least two more hours, but no one seemed to mind. Finally our beige, wood-paneled station wagon appeared. I could make out Dad in the driver's seat, but not so much Mom next to him. Everyone whooped and hollered as the car pulled into the driveway. I crawled underneath the crowd to reach the door just as it was opening, and there he was, Curtis Matthew, pink and puffy and so much tinier than I had expected from all the talk on the porch earlier: "Oh my God, eleven pounds," and "That's the biggest I ever heard," and "Poor Mary Ellen" (my mother).

Draped in light blue crepe paper, the porch held a bassinet overflowing with pillows and surrounded by flowers cut from all neighboring front yards. This was the biggest and best neighborhood event, rivaling even the Fourth of July picnic. Mothers sat on the porch swing and folding chairs, passing Curtis from one to another all day long. My grown-up brothers and friends, all of four and five years, played in our front yard, running up to the porch every ten minutes to take another look at the bundle that kept a dozen moms busy for a good six hours. My little brother spent his entire first day home on that front porch. I could not have been more proud.

We moved far away from Iris Avenue later that year and I have trouble remembering anything about the house, but I know that front porch, with its three steps and stone pillars, as if my baby brother had come home to it only yesterday. Today, when I drive through small towns with my family and friends, I point out each house I want to live in, visit, or convert into an inn. The common denominator in all my choices seems to be the front porch.

Helen's front porch is as much the reason she is the photographer for this book as her brilliant work. When I saw pictures of where she lived, I knew I had met a kindred soul. For me, the essential element of the front porch is comfortable seating. Two wicker rocking chairs facing out, a porch swing facing in, or a glider moving back and forth are balm to a family's soul. Helen had converted an old iron child's bed into the perfect spot to sip iced tea or nap on a summer afternoon. The wicker chairs and faded floral pillows were dangerously inviting.

We had so much fun adding garden accents to this idyllic spot. We had thought of hanging sap buckets filled with lobelia from the pillars of the porch, but the day before we were to put them up, I had a better idea: little urinals from an old hotel in France. I have a friend who scours Europe for unique containers and furniture for my work. She had brought these urinals back a couple of years ago, and I adored them. Many customers had admired them in the shop but just could not bring themselves to purchase them when they learned their original use. It was not until Helen came along, with a great sense of humor, and a family of all boys, that they finally found their proper new home.

As a photographer, Helen is particularly aware of and sensitive to light. She loves using candles, but had given up the fight with the wind on her porch. She had tried hurricane glass covers, but they were just not practical with kids around because they tipped over so

A PARADE
FOR MY BABY BROTHER CURT TO OUR PORCH

LEFT and ABOVE: A spontaneous parade erupted on Iris Avenue in 1963: a happy mom, a proud dad, and a protective big sister (me) kept Curtis on the front porch for his entire first day home. FOLLOWING PAGES: This two-hundred-year-old farmhouse had a stone porch that needed the warmth and ease of slipcovered pieces. The old iron child bed made an ideal couch. The gray-and-white-striped fabric is waterproof so the cushions can remain outside all summer.

THE **PORCH** IS
WHERE THE HEART IS

PORCH PERFECT

Some helpful hints for planting a porch container garden:

1. Use lots of the same plant rather than lots of different plants.

2. Choose one color or two complementary colors only.

3. Overplant your containers from the beginning. The more the flowers push out and trail down over the container, the better. A very full planting will also shield the soil from the sun, holding in moisture longer.

4. Plant in plastic containers first and then place these into more attractive containers. Plastic will hold the water longer.

5. Always water at night so that the roots have a long moist time before the sun hits them and dries them up.

6. Do not stop watering just because water is coming out of the bottom of the pot soon after you start. This usually means the plant is so dry that water is pouring through the soil like it's a colander. Only after the soil has been watered for several minutes will it start retaining the moisture like a sponge.

7. Feed your porch annuals once a week with a bloom booster from May through September. Everyone will ask you why your petunias look so much better than theirs.

8. Deadhead like crazy. The more you pinch back the dying blossoms before they go to seed, the more your annuals will bloom.

easily and cost plenty to replace. After I suggested she try mason jars, she sent me some pictures. It turns out her sister-in-law is a big canner and had a whole cellar full of chipped old jars with lids that no longer held their seal. So if you happen by Helen's house at night now, the candlelight will surely be burning, wind or no wind.

When designing plantings for a front porch, my motto is: less is more. Use very few varieties of plants. One kind of petunia, or verbena or impatiens, repeated throughout is a guaranteed hit. My Aunt Ruth Ann has planted red geraniums in fifteen or so containers on her wraparound porch by the beach for forty years. The white clapboard house, dark green shutters, and red geraniums are simply perfection. On any given summer day a car might slow down and shoot—picture perfect!

The biggest problem with the front-porch garden is that if it is designed for ultimate comfort, it becomes much easier to nap than to water. But plants in small containers need constant watering. My aunt waters four to five times a day in midsummer, because the sea breeze, salt air, and hot sun can be a deadly combination if she is not diligent.

I INHERITED A MESS

A good half of my business is reshaping a garden that already exists. Sometimes I am grateful for the existing plant material, containers, and architectural elements I have to work with. But more often than not, the garden is just an overwhelming mess. It can be a daunting task to look at lots of overgrown shrubs, trees, and weeds and try to imagine a beautiful garden.

Whether you find yourself looking at a mess of your own creation or someone else's, do not despair. Do resist the temptation that seems to afflict men in particular, of awakening early one Saturday morning and, with a chain saw, leveling everything in sight by noon. As satisfying as it may feel at the time, the devastation that remains will likely make matters far worse.

Instead, begin by laying out a step-by-step plan. If your trees need to

PREVIOUS PAGES: The decorative pillows transfer easily from living room to porch, as do Mark and the kids. Leave it to photographer Helen to devise a beautiful light source from candles in mason jars. And they won't blow out!

be pruned and your porch floor needs a coat of polyurethene and your yew has completely encroached upon your perennial bed, set some priorities. Start with the things that will give you the most visual satisfaction the quickest. Trim back the taxus first with hedge clippers. If, after cutting the shrub back, you still hate it, take it out. If the shrub looks much better but the trimming has exposed how bad the perennial garden looks, proceed with caution. Even if your instinct tells you to rip every perennial out, don't. Remove the weeds first, then cut out any dead stuff on the remaining plants. Step back. If it looks better, consider adding a mass of one kind of plant in the bare spaces before pulling out much more.

If there is a tremendous variety of flowering stuff in your garden, add a uniform covering plant. Lots of lavender or catnip planted throughout the entire garden just might tie all the disparate elements together. Once the new plants have gone in, step back and look again. If the garden still looks messy, there may just be too many different plant varieties for the space to appear unified. Now it is time to be ruthless and eliminate some plants because of the jumble of color. This narrowing of the color palette is the single most important factor in pulling a garden design together.

Determine what color is the most prominent, or the one you like the best, or the one you have most of. Once your primary or dominant color is chosen, all the other colors must complement it. My favorite gardens are simply slight variations of one color. Slight changes in hues add depth to a garden, whereas many colors fighting for attention add only confusion.

If you have lots of colors in your garden mess, start pulling out one color at a time. Go slowly. It is a lot easier to pull out than add back. Besides, you may discover a beautiful color combination emerging as you go along.

Once you are sure that what you have left in your garden is what you want to keep, take an overview. Are there any big showy blooms left? Are all the plants one height? Will things bloom throughout the summer or will everything bloom the first week in June and be done by July? Is there too much ground showing?

When in need of some real show-offs, delphiniums, TOP, and hollyhocks, ABOVE, offer spectacular color, tremendous height, and very little maintenance, as long as they can be protected from the wind.

If there are still a few elements to work out in the garden, remember what a mess you started with. Take some pride in what you have accomplished so far. If you have several priorities for your garden, try combining their solutions. For instance, if there are no big flowers *and* you need some height, plant some big clumps of delphinium or hollyhocks to solve both problems. Or if you need a ground cover *and* some spring bloomers, plant a perennial phlox.

Now that your perennial garden is gorgeous, take another look at the yew. Likely it, too, will have to go now and a magnificent hydrangea or lilac will be the only thing that will do your new little Eden justice. Finally, it is time to relax and hire someone to paint your deck and trim your trees. You can only be expected to do so much!

FROM EYESORE TO EYE-CATCHING

Years ago, my dear friend David received his first big bonus and decided to hire a designer to transform his apartment from early-dorm style into an elegant bachelor's pad. He asked a well-known store for a recommendation, and they set him up with an in-house design staff. The result: an apartment that was an expensive showcase for the store, with little personality. To this day, if you say the word "designer" to David, he breaks out in hives.

When Sharon and Carl Kess called Potted Gardens to redo their newly designed garden, I was reminded of David's excruciating realization that he had spent all his money on furniture he would never be comfortable sitting on. The Kesses had hired a local nursery to design and install their garden, and they hated it.

All too often, nurseries will provide design and installation services for customers who do not have the time or knowledge to do the initial work.

The ugly 1950s Plexiglas railing, ABOVE, nearly disappeared when we hung old ceiling tiles in front of the panels, RIGHT. And by moving the heavy trellising juniper to the brick wall, we made way for airier, more beautiful perennials and flowering annuals.

Some nurseries have excellent designers and experienced plantsmen who can put together a dynamite garden, while others use this service more as a selling outlet for their nursery's current stock. The advantage in hiring a designer who is not affiliated with any one nursery is that there is no limit to the choices of materials the designer may use. At Potted Gardens, we use as many as forty different suppliers in any given season. We are constantly on the lookout for new, better, less expensive resources. Some nurseries do give their staff designers free rein to use other resources whenever appropriate. If you are considering hiring someone to design and install your garden, make sure they have a wide network of resources and the permission to use them.

When I first saw the Kesses' newly designed garden, I knew which nursery had installed it. It was a place that specializes in hardy evergreens for container gardening. The entire garden was an odd assortment of bulky junipers and boxwoods planted in cedar boxes that looked too small. The design had no grace or soft edges, and there was barely a flower in sight.

The Kesses' terrace was a narrow cement balcony with a steel and Plexiglas railing that they hated. They were not permitted to change the street-side facade in any way, so one challenge was to draw attention away from this fifties-style material and create the distressed country look that they loved. Boxy espalier junipers, chosen by the first designer, were a rather inelegant solution that drew more attention to the Plexiglas panels and also blocked a spectacular city view.

I suggested wiring old tin ceiling tiles on the inside of the railing. Sharon was not so sure about them when I

The whole garden was transformed by adding cheery perennials such as coreopsis, LEFT, and nicotiana, ABOVE. The texture of the tin tiles was the perfect backdrop for the bark of the cherry tree as well.

described the idea, but once they were all hung, they became her favorite element in her new garden.

The espalier junipers were moved away from the railings, where they blocked the view, and placed in front of the tan painted brick wall of the building, which suited them much better. A looser, more natural border was created along the railing by using a variety of containers to hold a mix of annuals and perennials. Grasses and brooms added a windswept feel that also helped soften the outside steel-and-Plexiglas edge.

We kept most of the plants that had been introduced by the nursery. Some were plants I rarely choose, but I welcomed the opportunity to expand our repertoire. The Kesses had spent their entire garden budget on the first designers, so we tried to keep the expenses low for this second go-round. We simply rearranged most of what was there and added key new elements. Within two or three days, the balcony was completely transformed into an urban oasis. A week after the garden was planted, it looked as if it had been there for years.

Another client of ours, Leonard, had hired the same nursery two years before to design and plant the large terrace off his nineteenth-floor Manhattan condominium. Unlike the Kesses, he had chosen the nursery because they specialized in evergreens. His primary instruction to them was that he wanted a garden that would stay green all year, and he got just what he asked for. Large yews, boxwood, holly, blue spruce, Leyland cypress, and junipers were planted snugly into wooden boxes that were custom built to line the entire perimeter of the large terrace. The result was an overpowering green wall that completely blocked a terrific city view.

A mass planting of one kind of flower makes a much bolder statement than a mishmash of too many different species. My personal favorites are the prairie flowers, such as echinacea and rudbeckia, ABOVE and RIGHT.

When Leonard and I first met, he could not put his finger on exactly what he did not like about his garden. The trees were all beautiful and they were exactly what he had requested. As it was summer, all the boxes were underplanted with impatiens, which were blooming in a profusion of color, just as he wished. But the garden was neither beautiful nor peaceful. It was dense and claustrophobic.

What had happened to Leonard and his garden is common. When designing a garden, people tend to think only of the plants. Many begin with the wish to have lots of color *or* lots of flowers. Some, like Leonard, want to enjoy their garden year-round, so they assume it must consist entirely of evergreens. I shared with Leonard my belief that deciduous trees and shrubs offer an architectural beauty even after their leaves fall off. Besides, they never fully block the view.

Fortunately, Leonard had a second terrace area that had not yet been touched. We moved most of the evergreens to this new area, which could not be seen from the inside of the apartment, where the view had been so severely missed. On the main terrace we replaced the evergreens with a dozen clump and single birch trees and large sprawling spireas. We nestled dozens of large terra-cotta and galvanized containers in front of the wooden boxes to break up the linear monotony. We planted a profusion of monarda that would begin blooming just as the spirea faded. The garden was transformed from a pine forest into a perennial paradise with a magnificent city view!

Louis's spectacular twenty-story-views were once hidden by thick evergreens. We moved them to the back of the terrace while planting airier birch trees along the edges, ABOVE, and plenty of spirea in smaller pots for a lighter, cozier feel, LEFT and FOLLOWING PAGES.

DESI

GNING YOUR GARDEN

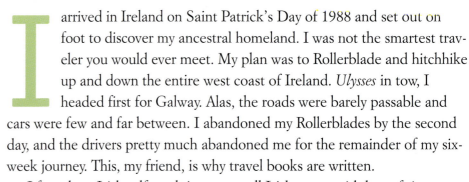

I arrived in Ireland on Saint Patrick's Day of 1988 and set out on foot to discover my ancestral homeland. I was not the smartest traveler you would ever meet. My plan was to Rollerblade and hitchhike up and down the entire west coast of Ireland. *Ulysses* in tow, I headed first for Galway. Alas, the roads were barely passable and cars were few and far between. I abandoned my Rollerblades by the second day, and the drivers pretty much abandoned me for the remainder of my six-week journey. This, my friend, is why travel books are written.

I found my Irish self stuck in very small Irish towns with lots of time on my hands. So, I wandered. I wandered through the sheep and cow fields, over stone walls, and across small brooks and streams. Seeing no one, I walked for hours every day. I had no travel book, no guide, no earthly idea where I was. At times even the century became blurred.

One day, in the middle of miles of sheep pastures, I stumbled upon a massive circular stone structure, a kind of tower, like nothing I had ever seen. This magnificent structure was fully intact on the outside. Along the inside walls, I could clearly see where an enormous spiral staircase had once climbed three levels, landing on floors that must have been two feet thick. There were a dozen tiny windows only wide enough to allow a man to shoot an arrow at an enemy across the River Shannon. Upon inquiry at the local pub that evening, I learned that this twelfth-century piece of history now served as a shelter for sheep on windy days.

Two days later, in Dingle, I stumbled upon sea caves that show themselves only at low tide. There were no markings or plaques to inform the foot traveler that these treacherous crevices had been chosen by her sister to be Marie Antoinette's accommodations had she not refused to flee her beloved France and lost her head. If not for my personal historian, disguised as a shepherd that day, I would never have known.

Why can't the overhead compartments on return flights to the United States hold olive jars from Crete, LEFT, iron urns from Provence, ABOVE, and spectacular views from Florence, RIGHT? I suppose our memories and photos, FOLLOWING PAGES, have to suffice to inspire us to create our own piece of paradise in our backyards.

HISTORY, NOT FLAUNTED, NEVER HIDDEN . . . IT'S JUST THERE

In Ireland one simply lives with history. It is not flaunted, never hidden, not even much liked. It is just there.

The Tuscan Italian countryside is much the same. A walk in an olive grove can be a far better history lesson than a guidebook's on the fall of the Roman Empire. These two landscapes also offer wonderful lessons in garden design. Ireland and Italy are renowned for their beauty, and this reputation comes as much from their hills and trees as it does from their old architectural remnants. When I design a garden, I imagine the most beautiful places I have ever seen, and these places are rarely gardens; they're the seacoast of Ireland, the hills surrounding Florence, and the lakes in New Hampshire. These places reveal exquisite partnerships between beauty and man. It is this beauty that calls to me when I stay away too long. It is their design I imagine when I attempt each new garden.

A SIMPLE SKETCH

I approach a garden the way a painter approaches a canvas. Usually, though not always, I will make a crude sketch of what the garden might look like. I draw every tree and all the containers and any furniture or architectural elements. I do not draw every plant, nor do I use any color in my drawings. From this simple sketch I make a list of the number and types of plants and containers I will need.

Like a painter, I do not know exactly what my garden will look like until I am well into the project, keeping open all possibilities. I find rigid drawings indicating the precise position of every plant too limiting.

Once my initial drawing is complete, I bring everything I need to the garden location. I like to have every container, every plant, all the soil and the furniture readily available from the beginning. I need to see how each

The back alleys of city townhouses can evoke memories of Italy with the right chandelier and trellis, LEFT. A two-hundred-year-old dugout canoe served as inspiration for this terrace design, TOP. Before I begin, I place every plant in every pot and stand back, RIGHT. If it's not right, I do it all again.

element works with the others before it is planted. It is important to see how large wooden containers look next to a flowery iron chair. This way I can change things as I go. Much like painting, creating a garden is best done in layers.

THE IMPORTANCE OF PLACEMENT

The correct placement of plants, furniture, and architectural elements can make or break a garden. I find it is best to begin by placing a tree or a large architectural element, one of your garden's "bones," in the corner that is most prominent from both inside the home and outside. In another corner, place your next largest plant or container, for balance. A third substantial plant or architectural element should be placed so as to form a triangle with your first two pieces. If you were to look at your garden from above, you would see a triangle formed by the two containers in the corners and one just off center facing them. From this simple triangle a garden begins.

The next step is to place elements around the three main pieces, making little garden areas. Continue to work in triangles, stepping the triangles down as you spread out from your bones. In other words, if your tree container is twenty-four inches tall, place an eighteen-inch container on one side of it and a fourteen-inch container on the closest other edge, creating your next triangle. Then place two smaller containers in the same manner around the eighteen-inch pot. Do the same with the fourteen-inch pot, until the desired area is covered. If you have three major areas, make them all a bit different in size and number of containers for a more natural look.

Once all the elements are placed in their general area, I step back and look. I look for a long time before I start moving things again. Then the

ABOVE: I like to begin with furniture placement when working in small spaces. RIGHT: And then by simply repeating one main plant like maiden grass throughout, a wonderfully sunny garden is created in an afternoon.

tweaking begins—a chair, a spirea, a statue moved slightly or eliminated altogether. I find I can tie the whole look together better if I move around the garden rather than staying to finish one section before beginning another.

As in a painting, color, texture, shape, light, and movement are the essential elements in garden design. If the upper right corner of the painting has a bold color, the lower left will need a strong element to provide balance. The same principle holds for gardening. If a painting is rich with beautiful color but its shapes are not effective, the painting will not work. And any great painting in a hideous frame or illuminated by a bare fluorescent bulb will lose 80 percent of its charm. The best way to ensure that all the elements are working well together is to have them all together from the beginning.

CREATING A CONTAINER GARDEN

If you are creating a potted garden, first position all the containers and then begin putting the plants inside each, leaving them in their nursery pots. Continue to work in triangles as each plant is positioned inside each container. For example, for a container with a twenty-four-inch opening, three to nine perennials may fit, depending on the size of their root balls. If you are working in triangles, you will always have an odd number of plants in each pot. Disregard the spacing instructions that come with each plant. These instructions will promote

LEFT: Old wooden ammunition boxes planted with sedum create a country feel. RIGHT and ABOVE: Vary the height and shape of metal containers such as feeding troughs, corner sinks, and old wash tubs for a cohesive, natural look.

maximum growth for plants in the ground, which is not always a good thing in a container.

Position three similar plants in a triangle pattern in your container. In a sunny garden you might use three rudbeckias first. If there is a lot of room left over, place two smaller perennials, such as lavender, around one of the rudbeckias. Continue this pattern until the container is full.

It is enormously helpful as you position your containers, plants, and furniture to continue to step back and look at your new garden. Remember, we are just placing plants in pots. It is not yet time to plant them in any soil. You will want to make sure your plants will evenly fill all your garden areas. If you notice that the big showy perennials are all on one side and the delicate wispy plants are on the other, you can still easily move things around because they are not yet planted. Once all your trees and perennials are in place, separate your flats of annuals into color groups while keeping each individual plant in its own little container. Mixing different annuals in one container is not nearly as effective as sticking to one variety per pot. Underplant masses of lobelia in one container and Swan River daisies in another. For any one porch, patio, or terrace, select no more than three annuals that all work well together.

Once all the placement decisions have been made and viewed, the planting can begin. If all the containers and garden areas are prepared ahead of time, progress should advance rather quickly from here on. Planting is a little like kneading dough—the longer you work it, the tougher it gets. Begin with the largest plants. You may have to move the smaller ones away in order to have the space to work, but keep them together in position elsewhere so they can easily be added back as you need them. If the larger containers need more plants than originally thought, steal from the smaller ones and eliminate some containers.

Plant each container much as you would a natural border. The taller plants should be more to the back, and as you move toward the front of the pot, the plants should be lower. Squash the impulse to plant one tall dracaena in the middle, then circle it with geraniums and edge with vinca. There is nothing natural about this design. Instead, be creative and remember the triangles. When one container is planted, place a smaller one up against the completed one so the two will work together. Continue patterns of height and color in each newly nestled pot.

Remain flexible as you work your way around the garden. Some plants will not work where you had hoped and other areas will need more or less than you anticipated during your placement exercise.

COLOR AND FORM

The most important element of a great garden design, for me, is color. A magnificent structural design can be ruined by clashing blossoms. And the messiest planting can be pulled together easily by eliminating all but one color. When imagining their garden, most people say they want lots of color. But lots of different colors can really detract from the elegance and peacefulness of a garden. Lots of one or two complementary colors are often much more effective. The impact of many shapes and sizes of one color will result in a colorful garden with tremendous impact.

If calm is the purpose of your garden, use a tight color

The shape and color of this old pink enamel pitcher, LEFT, made it too hard to resist at the town dump. And to think it was discarded for the holes that now give it perfect drainage! Keeping containers to a tight color palette of chocolates and rusts, RIGHT, makes the foliage of this sweet potato vine that much more delectable.

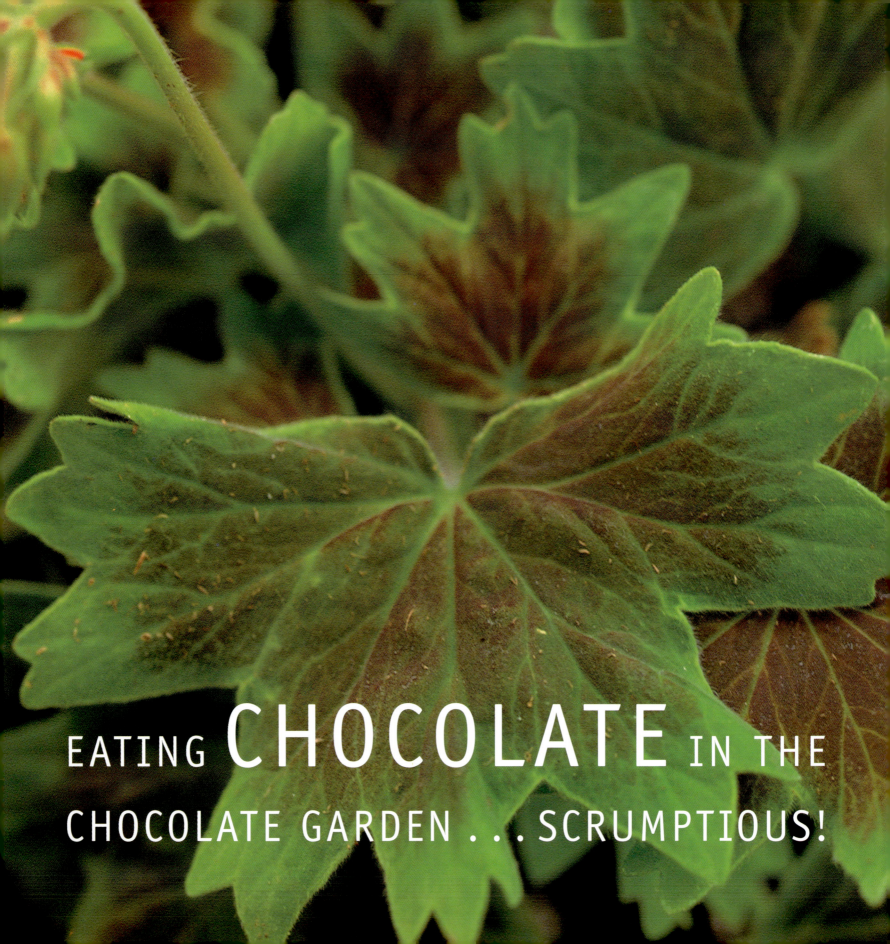

EATING **CHOCOLATE** IN THE

CHOCOLATE GARDEN . . . SCRUMPTIOUS!

palette. This is particularly important in a small space. A tight palette means only one or two colors. Once a third color is introduced to a small area, the space can begin to look cluttered.

If one color feels too limiting, look to one side of your main color on the color wheel. For instance, if red is your main color, add magenta, burgundy, and pink, from the blue side of red, *or* rust, orange, and blood-red from the yellow side of red. It is best not to combine one color from the yellow side and one from the blue; they can clash. If using varying hues of one color does not seem enough, add one complementary or accent color. To enjoy the garden at night, consider white as the accent to almost any color. At night white will seem to drink up the moon, and by day it highlights the color next to it. But remember that in gardening white is very much a color. It is not, as is often thought, neutral. The color white can be neutral in interior house painting; in gardening, however, it is a bold and bright color. Green is the only neutral color in the palette of any gardener.

I love to design gardens using unique and complementary plants and architectural pieces. Plant selections may be dictated by the color and shape of an architectural treasure. For example, old black cast-iron pieces invite rust- and chocolate-colored leaves as perfect companions. Sweet potato vine, heuchera, purple basil, and fountain grass make a scrumptious chocolate garden. Iron planters and statuary can hold equal status with these exquisite leaves, whereas the subtle changes in light and texture of the dark architectural pieces would be lost in a garden full of color.

When the right elements are chosen for a patio or porch, very little planting is needed to turn it into a little Eden. Simple complementary plantings alongside a unique piece of furniture or architecture can hold as much interest and delight as a large perennial border. Remember, the beauty of a garden lies as much in the form as in the color choices. The more sophisticated the design or the architectural element, the less is needed to make a powerful impact. For me, sophistication comes from a simple, focused concept: a massive planting of all one kind of rose, a wall of birch trees in galvanized tubs, or a cozy cluster of iron furniture with chocolate-colored plants.

One of my favorite examples of a sophisticated patio design is one we planted in shades of silver. The patio's slate floor inspired the design. We chose a collection of stone, concrete, and zinc barrels and galvanized buckets for planters. We used small silver birch trees for height, and every planter was overflowing with wonderful combinations of silver and blue lobelia, lamb's ears, morning glories, artemisia, salvia, borage, lavender, and catnip. The furniture consisted of new cedar benches that weathered to a grayish silver in a few months. An old gray painted bench doubled as both a coffee table and a footrest. Lanterns of tin illuminated the garden at night, and from the inside, a Victorian screen door with its original blue paint provided the perfect lens through which to view this silvery wonderland.

PREVIOUS PAGES: From the iron grapes of the bench to the deep burgundy leaves of heuchera, this whole garden seems edible! The silver-blue tone of lavender, lamb's ear, and artemisia echo the colors of the graystone planter, LEFT, and the old blue screen door, RIGHT.

USING HANGING PLANTS

After window boxes, the most frequent request from my urban customers is to incorporate hanging baskets. Since I have a tremendous aversion to plastic, I refuse to carry plastic hanging baskets in my store. There are not, however, many other ready-made choices. Moss-lined wire baskets are attractive, but I find they dry out too quickly to be really practical. So we have fashioned some hanging containers out of ordinary items.

One of my favorites is an old galvanized bucket. If the flowering plant is to be hung over an area that should not get wet, don't just decide not to drill a hole in the bottom of the bucket. Instead, keep the plant in an ugly plastic pot and hide it by plopping it into an attractive one. Every couple of waterings, take the container down and dump out any water that may have accumulated. No plant will survive with its roots sitting in water —unless, of course, it is a water plant.

Be creative with vessels for hanging—those plastic pots will never do! ABOVE: Cast-iron enameled-wall sinks from France make ideal containers for the wall. Simply plop the ugly plastic pot into the sink and let the beautiful ivy overflow the edges. LEFT: Lamb's ear and verbena make a striking combination, softening the chain in an old bucket.

DESIGNING WITH BULBS

Planting bulbs in any small space needs to be done carefully. Tulips, daffodils, and crocuses can offer a spectacular show while they are blooming, but remember that there is not much worth looking at when their blooms are spent. Most bulbs must be planted in the fall so they can have four to five months of cold to stimulate a spring show. Bulbs bloom only once a year.

When planting bulbs in a container, prepare the pot as you would for any other plant, with a drainage hole and a terra-cotta chip over it (see page 142). Then add a couple of inches of soil. For the most part, the bigger the bulb, the deeper it will need to be planted. Most daffodils are happy under ten inches of soil, so plant them first. Place the bulbs side by side till the container is covered. Throw two inches of soil over the daffodils and pat it down slightly. Next, place an entire layer of late-blooming tulips snugly together. Add a couple more inches of soil. Repeat the process for the crocuses, covering them with a couple of inches of soil firmly patted down. Water thoroughly and wait. Four months later the show will begin. Chosen properly, your pot could bloom continually for three months straight!

In the fall, plant bulbs in pots later than you would plant them in the ground —wait until mid-December for container planting, rather than late October,

which is customary for ground planting. Use a large pot if you plan to keep it outside all winter. If you have a cool, damp basement or garage in which to force bulbs, you can use smaller pots. Every container must have excellent drainage and will need to be kept moist (not wet) all winter. The most common problem with bulbs is rot, caused by lack of drainage and too much water. Another common bulb problem is the rapid freeze-and-thaw cycle caused by unpredictable winters. To help prevent damage from this type of weather, winterize your pots properly (see page 154). This will act as a kind of thermos to keep the soil from freezing or thawing too rapidly. The method is not foolproof, but it will significantly increase your chances of blossoms in the spring.

Plant bulbs right next to one another. Containers look best with an overcrowded profusion of blooms. Bulbs do not need the amount of space between them that is recommended on most packages. They do, however, need space beneath them for their roots to grow, but this is usually only a couple of inches. There are an infinite variety of bulbs, with a wide range of blooming schedules. Crocuses, muscari, and mini irises are famous for their very early arrival, often not waiting for the snow to melt. Daffodils traditionally come next,

LEFT and ABOVE: The key to planting bulbs in a container is to overplant. Layer bulbs according to size. In other words, put large daffodils on the bottom, tulips next, and crocuses last.

PACK THE SOIL WELL
AND WATER THOROUGHLY

followed by hyacinths, which arrive just in time for Easter. The beauty queens generally appear last, in the form of tulips. This is just a rough schedule, because within each variety there are early and late arrivals. Some bulbs even prefer to bloom in the fall rather than the spring. To get the most out of your bulbs, learn their precise arrival in your neck of the woods. To orchestrate a symphony of blooms, plant four or five different varieties of bulbs in the same pot by layering them from largest to smallest.

Bulbs come in an incredible range of colors. Though it is tempting to buy as many different colors as you possibly can, don't! These intense colors can clash with one another if you are not careful. Keep a tight rein on your rainbow and buy in bulk, because here again, masses of the same flower look much better than a potpourri.

After the blooms have finished, their leaves turn yellow and then brown and flop to the ground. It is at this homely stage that the bulb begins storing food for next year's show. Unless you plant new bulbs each year, you must leave the ugly leaves alone for at least a couple of weeks after they bloom.

In a small space you may want to dispense with these ugly sections altogether by digging up the bulbs right away and buying new ones every year. Most people, however, would call this an extremely wasteful gardening practice. One way to avoid both the waste and the ugly stage is to plant all your bulbs in a few easily movable pots. Place the pots prominently in your garden while the flowers are showing off. Once they begin to die back, move the entire pot to the rear of the garden or behind a fence. The bulbs still need to be watered and fed as their leaves yellow and brown, so take heed that out of sight does not become out of mind.

Perhaps the best method is the following: after the blossoms have come and gone and the leaves have died back sufficiently, the bulbs can be dug up and stored in a cool, dry, dark place until next fall, when they can be planted again. If you plan to use the same container for perennials, you may need to remove the bulbs in order to make room for them. You also stand better odds that most of your bulbs will bloom again if you remove them. The chances of bulbs rotting under too much water are high in a container of plants that will need a good drink daily throughout the summer.

It is easy to forget to water a pot that is not showing green. Remember that bulbs like to begin to grow in the moisture of early spring snow thaws.

PLA

NTING
AND MAINTAINING

The first step in choosing plants for your garden is determining what generally grows in your area. The resources for gaining this knowledge are endless. If you like doing research, you will do well on the Internet and in the library. The big problem with turning to books is that they generally can't be sufficiently specific about the plants that do well in your particular environment because they are usually sold nationally or internationally.

If you are more the visual type, you might need to see a plant in all its glory before you can place it in your garden. If you have not had the experience of growing certain plants, choose blooming plants from a nursery. Any good local, independently owned nursery will know which plants grow naturally in your area and which foreign species will adapt. Avoid the big chains selling rows and rows of the same plants at very low prices. These places purchase in bulk from one or two large growers, who are likely to be a thousand miles from your backyard. Though many plants will do well almost anywhere, plenty will not.

I recommend that novice gardeners buy their plants from local nurseries, not catalogs. Many of us have had the experience of ordering the beautiful plants pictured on the cover of a catalog, only to find they look nothing like that picture when planted in our own backyard. Direct-mail services tend to be nationally focused, and their goal is to sell the most plant material to the most people. There are some wonderful exceptions to this, but the direct contact and visual lessons you gain from a nursery are irreplaceable. Local nurseries *must* grow and sell plants that do well locally. Once you know what thrives in your garden, you can then use mail order as a great way to save money.

ABOVE: There is nothing simpler and more beautiful than a showy annual, like the scaevola, in a gorgeous pot. Water and, voilà!, watch it grow. RIGHT: Always check with the real experts—your local family-owned nursery—for what grows best in your neighborhood.

A PLANTING SCHEDULE

If you are a new gardener or have recently moved to a new zone, consider planting your garden in three stages. Folks below the Mason-Dixon line can start this plan just about any time. Northerners need to hold off until after the last expected chance of frost, usually in May.

First determine where your plants are going to go and how tall and wide your groupings should be. Go to a nursery and purchase only one-third of your garden from the plants that are looking good and full and are just about ready to bloom. Buy lots of only two or three species, and choose plants that are different sizes and shapes but all one color. Plant them in groups and repeat these clumps in a natural pattern throughout your garden space. Leave plenty of room for the next round of planting.

Six weeks later, return to the nursery. This time, again buy lots of two or three different plants. Keep with either the first color you chose or pick another color that complements it nicely. If purple was your spring color, yellow may be your early summer one. If you buy only the plants that are just now looking full and about to burst into bloom, you will have begun to create a cycle of blooming in your garden that will rival that of the most sophisticated horticulturists. Plant your new varieties in some but not all the spaces left from the last planting. Leave room for the next go-round.

In early September, head for the nursery again, where you will find asters just ready to burst. All the incredible fall foliage will begin to show, along with the wonderful berries on hundreds of shrubs. Again, buy only the few varieties that will complement your existing

If you are not sure of the color of a particular rose, buy the plant only when one is in bloom. RIGHT: If you love it, buy a lot of the same, but not enough to fill your garden. If you buy *all* your plants at the beginning of spring, based on what looks good at the nursery *then*, you won't have tall grasses blowing by midsummer, LEFT.

PLANT COUNT

Though there is no real formula for the ideal number and size of plants for the perfect garden, here are some good rules of thumb:

1. Plant trees in odd numbers (unless you are going for a completely classical garden, where everything is perfectly symmetrical and planted in pairs).

2. For every one tree, add one and a half shrubs, such as spirea or lilac, or large perennials, such as russian sage or catnip.

3. For every shrub, add three medium-sized perennials.

4. For every medium-sized perennial, add five times as many smaller perennials.

5. For every two square feet of space, under-plant one flat of annuals *or* three small perennials per container.

This formula is like a recipe: cooks who must measure each ingredient follow it exactly, but it will work just as well for those who like to use a recipe merely as a guide.

I don't like to begin a gardening project until I have assembled all my plants, containers, and furniture in front of me, RIGHT. I love the feeling of satisfaction when that big mess becomes a beautiful garden in just a few short hours!

garden. Remember to purchase in bulk, and this time take home enough to completely fill any holes in your garden.

When these fall bloomers are planted, you will have successfully created a continually blooming garden. And though it took an entire growing season to get it all in, you will have your garden for years to come. You won't be ripping out ugly surprises later on because you knew what you were getting all along.

A CONTAINER-GARDEN SHOPPING LIST

To begin a potted garden, determine the number of containers you will need. Separate your containers by size and shape when counting them. Every tree gets its own large container. Every large perennial or shrub gets its own medium container. I like to plant in groupings of various containers, where every large pot will be surrounded by at least five medium to small ones. If the space is large, you may need as many as fifteen containers surrounding any one tree.

Once you have counted the number of containers needed to create the look you want, it is time to count the plants. The trees are easy. The shrubs can be counted next. For a container garden, I would recommend staying away from dense, stiff shrubs. In my opinion, boxwood and holly look infinitely better in the ground than they do in a planter. Use squiggly, loose, airy shrubs to create a natural, flowing structure to your garden. Some of my favorites are the many varieties of spirea, cotoneaster, serviceberry (especially *Amelanchier arborea*), butterfly bush (*Buddleia*), bluebeard (*Caryopteris clandonensis*), Chinese witch hazel, flowering quince (*Chaenomeles japonica*), and barberry. As in all your plant choices, narrow things down to one or two varieties per size and species. Nature teaches us about the beauty of repetition. When you walk in the woods, for example, you will find hundreds of the same species of ferns, as far as the eye can see. Similarly, for your larger shrubs, instead of choosing one spirea, one lilac, two cotoneasters, and one euonymus, use five spireas. This unifies the garden.

COUNT THE CONTAINERS AND BUY ENOUGH

PLANTS TO **OVERSTUFF** THEM

PREPARING

All containers must have drainage holes to ensure the long, healthy life of a plant. You may hear a number of interesting ways to get around this requirement, but don't believe them.

1. Make a ½-inch hole for every square foot of bottom surface, with either a drill,

2. pruning shears to separate the slats between wooden planks, or

3. my personal favorite, the pick ax!

4. To keep the hole from clogging or losing soil, place a terra-cotta chip over the hole or

5. cut open an industrial-strength garbage bag and

6. line all wood and metal boxes, being careful not to cover the drainage holes with plastic.

7. Fill the container with a good potting soil and let the planting begin!

8. Once planting is completed, you can tuck the edges of the plastic into the soil.

HOW TO PLANT

Once you have purchased a healthy plant, it is important to plant it properly to ensure a long and healthy life. It is in the first two or three weeks after being introduced to its new home that most problems arise, so if you can give a plant a good start, you will be well on your way to a long-lasting garden.

Water your plants thoroughly when you bring them home from the nursery or receive them by mail. Try to put them in the soil within twenty-four hours of their arrival. This way the trauma they suffer in transportation will be shortened. However, the new trauma of transplanting will begin, so take special care.

A plant's roots should be thoroughly wet before they are covered with new soil. All the packaging that protects the roots should be carefully removed before you set the plant in the ground. If you are planting in containers, even biodegradable materials, such as burlap and paper pots, should be removed. These products will not have the benefit of ground worms to help break down their natural fibers, so, for example, any burlap wired around the root ball of a tree will remain for several years, eventu-

LEFT and ABOVE: I find that there is a delicate balance between handling plant material *too* gingerly and overworking it. Root balls must be loosened but not completely ripped apart. Make sure all newly planted roots are completely covered with fresh potting soil before adding decorative top elements like sand or mulch.

ally strangling the growing roots. Of course, removal of these protective cases should be done with caution, as they are generally holding the soil around the roots, and it is always best to keep this soil during transplanting.

Remove all dead or dying plant material from the plant. It is not uncommon to find dying leaves around the base of a new plant; as long as you have chosen a healthy-looking plant from a reputable local nursery or received a good specimen from a mail-order company, do not be alarmed by this. Simply remove anything that does not look perfect. A healthy start will ensure a healthy life.

Place the moist plant in the soil so that the top of the root ball is even with the level of the soil. Firmly pat down soil all around the plant so that no air pockets remain. Be careful not to "mound up" when planting. This occurs when a plant's root ball is higher than the level of the soil and can cause severe drought and wind problems, killing even the healthiest plants in the first week or two after transplanting. At the very least a plant situated this way will never thrive.

IRRIGATION SYSTEMS

All gardens need some kind of irrigation system or they just will not grow. The most common watering choices include Mother Nature, you and a hose, a well-placed sprinkler that you turn on when the garden looks dry, an automatic sprinkler, and a drip-irrigation system. If your garden is planted in the ground and you get excellent rainfall from spring through late fall, count your blessings and watch your garden grow. Nearly every other garden will require some amount of supplemental watering.

Do not make the common mistake of assuming that your container garden is getting sufficient water from a couple of good rainfalls. Plants in the ground can live for weeks on the moisture left in the soil long after a good rain, but plants in a container will suck all the moisture out of a container within hours or days, depending on heat and wind. Larger containers can go longer without watering than smaller ones, while some plants thrive in a draught and others will die within hours of too little water.

If you have a container garden, consider installing an irrigation system on a timer so you will not be tied to your garden all summer. Even gardeners need vacations. And as most mothers will attest, it is nearly impossible to find a good baby-sitter and none will ever replace you.

There was a time, only a few short years ago, when I did not recommend automatic irrigation systems. I found them to be unreliable, ugly, difficult to install, leaky, and a real pain to maintain. Then I met Declan Keane, and all that changed. If only I could clone him for every region in this country and abroad, then everyone could have the pleasure of his charming Irish lilt as he

IF YOU NEED AN IRRIGATION SYSTEM, I

explains how your newly installed system will work perfectly. Short of that, I will try to describe just what he does for all my container gardens in New York.

The premise of a drip-irrigation system is simple. A main hose (or two) will wrap around the entire perimeter of the garden. This hose is attached to an outdoor water spigot. A source of electricity is needed next to the hose for an automatic timer. The timer is then connected by an on/off switch to the main artery hose. Tiny rubber tubes are inserted into small, well-sealed holes throughout the main artery. Each potted container will receive at least one of these tiny tributaries, depending on the size of the container and the water requirements of the plant; some containers may need a dozen or more of these tiny hoses. Each small rubber vein can carry only so much water at a time. Adjustments can be made once a system is up and running by removing or adding the little hoses or by turning the system on less or more often if the entire garden looks too dry or too wet.

Some drip-irrigation systems come with attachments that you can place in the tips of the tributaries to regulate the water flow. These attachments look like tiny balls, small enough to move around but just large enough so they won't fall out of the end of the tiny hose. The idea is that any tributary hose without a little ball will let out more water than a tributary with a ball. In theory it sounds good, but I have found that in practice it seldom works properly. Those little balls inevitably get clogged with soil, and no water at all comes out of their hoses. I recommend the simple, more-or-fewer tributaries approach that Declan uses. It clogs a lot less.

ABOVE: Each tributary hose is attached to the main hose, which is attached to a timer, sending water precisely when and where it is needed. Some plants may need five tributaries while others only need one. Often a few weeks of trial and error are needed to get the proper amount of water to each plant. Never go on vacation the week after your irrigation system is installed. Wait at least a month.

RECOMMEND HIRING A PROFESSIONAL!

To prevent soil from clogging the little hoses, each should have a metal cap; these can be found in good nurseries and some hardware stores, along with the other supplies needed for your irrigation system. Secure the tributaries in place with curved metal stakes placed just a few inches from the tip of the small tube. Gently push the length of the tributary hose into the soil so its tip will rise slightly above the surface. Check the tips of your tributary hoses often. They can get clogged and flop out of the pot. Be particularly diligent before that big family vacation. You do not want to ruin it by returning to a dead garden.

Adjust the timer setting as the seasons change. Remember, container gardens need more water than in-the-ground gardens. In the early spring you may need the system to go on every three days for twenty minutes at a time. If you just planted many of your containers, they will require more water more often, perhaps every two days for thirty minutes. As the days grow longer and hotter, you will need to turn up the water flow, perhaps up to twenty minutes every day until the middle of the summer. Scorching July and August heat may require as much as thirty minutes twice a day.

It is usually better to water less often but for a longer time than to give your garden lots of little drinks. Plants can lose their ability to drink if they do not begin to dry out between each watering. You can check the soil by sticking your finger down under the surface at least two inches; if it still feels damp that far down, do not water yet.

Water your outdoor plants in the evening so that the roots will enjoy a long cool drink throughout the night. If you water in the morning, the sun could dry out the soil before the roots even get their first sip. If your garden needs to be watered twice a day, do it at midday and midnight. Of course, if your watering system is you and a hose, work it around your schedule. You are, after all, more important than your plants.

Container gardens are not the only ones that will benefit from an automatic irrigation system. Simple soaker hoses and sprinklers can easily be set on timers to go on in the middle the night or the middle of your vacation. Soaker hoses slowly ooze water out of a porous rubber tube, instead of holding it in. They are great for wetting just the soil around your plants, rather than everything else in your garden. Some towns regulate against garden irrigation systems because of the misguided notion that the automatic ones waste a lot of water.

In my experience, the manual method can be far less efficient. Manual hoses and movable sprinklers waste water by spraying all over the place. With a regulated timer you can give your garden exactly the water it needs, no less and, more important, no more. Of course, if there is a drought in your area, do not water. It is much easier to replace a plant than a town's water supply.

The most important factor in choosing the right watering system for your garden is to have selected appropriate plants for your area. If you live in the desert, do not try to grow roses, and if you live in Maine, do not grow cacti. Do some research on which plants are indigenous to your region and use them extensively.

LEFT: Nothing beats an old-fashioned watering can. If you want to cover a wall quickly with vines, use beans. Scarlet runner beans, RIGHT, are one of my favorites. They grow like weeds and can cover a large space in weeks. Since they need to be planted each year, also plant slow-growing ivy that will cover the same wall after five or six years.

CHOOSING THE RIGHT PLANT FOOD

All plants need fuel to survive. A plant's fuel comes from the sun, the water, and the soil. The main nutrients needed for proper plant growth are nitrogen, phosphorous, and potassium. Powdered plant foods will break down the percentage of these three important ingredients in alphabetical order on their packaging. In other words, if the food contains 25 percent nitrogen, 50 percent phosphorous, and 25 percent potassium, the package would read 25-50-25.

Learning what each nutrient provides for a plant will help you garden more effectively. Any container garden must have a regular feeding program to continue blooming. In-the-ground gardens rarely receive every nutrient in the exact balance needed, so a little help never hurts them as well.

Nitrogen stimulates leaf growth and vegetation. All your evergreens, trees, and berried shrubs will benefit from some additional nitrogen. Herbs and vegetables need regular doses to produce generous harvests.

Phosphorous promotes flowers. For flower gardens, regular feedings of phosphorous-rich plant food are essential to colorful, large, and long-lasting blossoms.

Potassium encourages strong root growth. Trees, shrubs, vines, and roses will be healthier if they begin life with strong roots. My grandfather buried banana peels around the bases of all his roses early each fall. The results were strong, long-lasting roses.

For flowering gardens, buy a plant food with a high middle number. Feed your plants

Most plants will do well with a generic balanced plant food that reads 30-30-30 on its package. However, for more, longer-lasting, and brighter flowers in containers, I use a bloom booster with more phosphorous and therefore a higher middle number.

half the recommended dose if you have a container garden. Always add plant food to well-watered plants. Heavy doses of these nutrients on dry roots or stems can burn the plants. Do not use chemically made plant food in places where it can seep into the water supply.

WRAPPING FOR THE WINTER

When I lived in Chicago in the seventies and early eighties, I would prepare my body and soul for the long winters by wrapping my hundred-year-old windows with plastic, buying a new comforter for the couch, and stocking up on a dozen fat books. People hibernate in Chicago, bears hibernate in New Hampshire, and gardens hibernate north of the Mason-Dixon line. Winterizing your garden will make this less traumatic for your plants.

Containers made of terra-cotta, natural woods, and metal will also get damaged if they are not treated properly. If you live in an area that gets any kind of sustained freezing temperatures, you will have to choose your containers and plants carefully and do some simple things to prepare them for winter. Although containers are increasingly being made out of plastics so they won't crack, I still prefer the natural materials. A plastic terra-cotta-

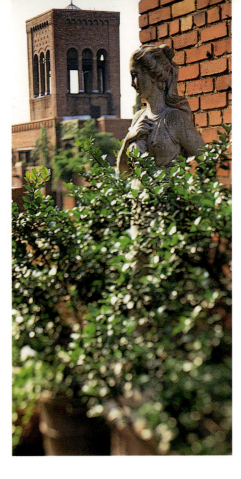

look pot, no matter how well it is made, will never equal the natural beauty of clay. But clay pots crack in the winter because they are porous; water gets trapped in these imperceptible air holes and then freezes, expands, and cracks the pot. The higher the temperature in the kiln during the firing of these pots, the smaller the air holes and the lower the chances of breakage. Some clay pots will advertise this high-temperature advantage and even guarantee their pots

Most stone and cement planters can withstand typical northern winters, although severe weather could wreak havoc on them over time. My approach to stone containers is "live and let live." They are too heavy to move in and out or even to lift and wrap. If a stone container cracks, I'll mend it as best I can and plant some moss in the crack.

EASY
WINTERIZING

The life of both plants and pots can be prolonged in northern climates by winterizing.

1. Wrap bubble wrap around the sides of all terra-cotta pots and any small wood and metal pots. Do not cover the bottom of the pots because water must be able to drain out of them.

2. For each pot, cut two pieces of thirty-six-inch-wide burlap into strips long enough to cover the pot. Then crisscross the two strips of burlap and place the container upright in the center of the X.

3. Pull up the ends of the burlap.

4. For odd-shaped pots, sew the top with twine using the type of large needle that nurseries use for sewing burlap around the root ball of large shrubs and trees.

5. Tighten the burlap securely over the top of the pot.

6. Tie off the end with a sewing knot.

7. Elevate all the wrapped pots off the ground by two inches to ensure proper drainage.

8. Snuggle the pots together so they can protect one another from the harsh winter winds. If you have a wall or fence, place the pots behind it.

from breaking. These pots usually cost more, but considering that many cheaper pots will break each year, they can be worth the investment.

Some wooden containers are prone to rotting if they are not treated with a waterproofing process. The chemicals used in this process, however, can be toxic to both children and plants. Some woods, such as teak, cedar, and redwood, naturally hold up to water better than others, and many planters and decks are made out of these woods. But after visiting the diminishing redwood forests in California, I no longer use or recommend the latter.

When I first began planting container gardens, I did very little to prepare them for the variable winters of New York, and so the plants suffered from the continual freeze-and-thaw cycles. The temperature on one January day might be fifteen degrees, and the next day it would get up to sixty degrees. This rapid shift in temperature would really wreak havoc on plants and pots. Much to my chagrin, I lost half my containers and a third of the plants each season. Considering what was spent on both, this was not a good rate of return. I had to invent a method of protecting both containers and plants from wind, snow, and ice. The method I came up with is not foolproof, but it has reduced my breakage and plant loss to less than 10 percent.

The burlap adds an attractive natural cover to the plastic bubble wrap. North of Virginia, terra-cotta pots need to be protected from the cold.

FURNITURE AND AR A

DDING
CHITECTURAL ELEMENTS

When I was fourteen, my friends all hung out at the shopping mall. The mall ritual always bored me. My idea of a good time, even as a teenager, was to go antiquing. Luckily, we lived in Wexford, Pennsylvania, a town known more for its antique stores than its malls. I bought my first old cupboard when I was sixteen. Frankly, I think my mother worried about this behavior far more than if I had hung out at the mall with my friends. Looking back, she was right to worry. My odd adolescent interest was a premonition of a serious addiction to come.

I am sure my entire business today is a pretext for my antique obsession. I love buying old things! I love everything about it: the country auctions, the dusty antique stores, the open-air flea markets. When I go to an auction or a flea market and find some wonderful thing, I buy it. I often have no idea exactly how I am going to use it. But I know I must have it!

I used to buy so much I would have to rent a U-Haul trailer every time I ventured out. Like the practitioner of any discipline (and I am using the term loosely), I have honed my skills and now buy only the gems of the market. I buy only if I need it *today* or if it is so beautiful or unique, I know I will find a way to use it tomorrow. But I must warn you, it took me years and many expensive mini-storage bills to learn auction discretion.

Today when I find some wonderful piece, I put it in my wonderful-piece storage room (also known as my living room) and live with it for a while, until its mysteries reveal themselves to me. In doing so, I have realized that I collect things in waves. When I buy one rusty black iron statue, I then seem to run into many other rusty black iron pieces—an urn, a planter, a bench, and so on.

LEFT: Look for simple lines when hunting for old metal and wooden garden furniture. ABOVE: I've got a real thing for birdbaths and candles. These floating rose candles, sprinkled with cinnamon to look antique, are the perfect touch to a garden party at dusk.

ABOVE: The day I found this swing, originally from a park in Paris and brought here by a kindred soul, I knew my garden was complete. RIGHT: The size and comfort found in 1940s "bouncy chairs" is not often present in new garden furniture.

CHOOSING FURNITURE

Clearly I have a weakness for old garden furniture. I even like it indoors. My bedroom in the country faces the mountains, and there is no better viewing spot for them than inside, from my old painted Adirondack chair.

When I design a garden, I like to know what furniture will be used before I make a plan. Many of my clients allow me to choose the furniture for them after I explain how essential it is to the overall garden design. Over the years, it has become increasingly difficult to find good old garden furniture, but to me there is nothing better. Although some new garden furniture designs are attractive, there is rarely a leaf pattern or a hinge that can rival the work found on an original 1920s or '30s piece of ironwork. Fortunately, not everyone shares my passion for the old, so you can still get some good deals on entire furniture sets at tag sales.

Furniture can determine the overall look and feel of a garden. A nineteenth-century iron Philadelphia bench can turn an average garden into one fit for a king. Plastic lawn chairs can do more harm to the look of a perennial border than a hundred weeds. Choose furniture that fits your lifestyle and looks great. If sunbathing is your thing, find old lounge chairs at a flea market and recover them in a waterproof fabric so you can leave the cushions outside when it

I OFTEN BEGIN MY GARDEN DESIGNS WITH THE FURNITURE I FIND

rains. If eating alfresco is your passion, there is nothing better than a big old harvest table with mismatched chairs under an arbor of grapevines.

Most old cushions are worthless by the time you buy the piece, so I prefer furniture that does not require cushions; they are a real hassle to make and even more of a problem to store if you have very little space. If you do want cushions, you must use waterproof fabric if you plan to leave them outdoors all summer. And remember how easy it is to forget to bring them all in every time it rains! The difficulty comes with finding attractive waterproof material. Not surprisingly, I love the old faded flowers or stripes that are rarely found in waterproof fabrics. The best solution is to work with the canvaslike fabric that is used to make awnings and table umbrellas, either in solids or simple stripes. There's nothing worse than sitting on a sticky plastic seat in the hot sun or the humid evening air, so I do not recommend the shiny plastic fabric sold in limited colors at most fabric

stores. There is a waterproofing finish that can be added to any fabric, but it too is shiny; it's great for tablecloths, but not for seats.

Boat upholstery fabric is another terrific solution. I often take my garden furniture to a shop where boat cushions are recovered. The choice of colors and designs is still limited, but you can usually find classic fabrics meant for use on fine boats. A basic off-white goes with anything and detracts from nothing. Insist on slipcovers; you can easily remove and wash them.

LEFT: This unique 1950s furniture set is a wonderful example of unforced elegance. ABOVE: Make seat cushions out of waterproof fabric so they can stay outdoors. Then add decorative pillows, usually kept indoors, when your guests arrive. Remember, the simpler the pattern on the seat cushions, the more they will accentuate the lines of the furniture.

WHAT TO LOOK FOR IN FURNITURE

It is always a little tricky to buy old furniture because there are two big reasons people throw something out: either they do not like it anymore or it is broken. The key to buying old garden furniture is to find things discarded only for the former reason, not for the latter.

Some of the best old garden furniture is made of iron. A lot of it can still be found in pretty great shape. I once found a set of iron furniture that was over two hundred years old and without a flaw. I had to pay a small fortune for the set, but it was utterly beautiful. The 1920s and '30s produced terrific-looking iron furniture that was solidly built. Art Deco influenced the designs, but they remain somewhat classic in feel. Among my favorite finds are the adjustable lounge chairs with big rolling wheels that were once pushed around by nurses for those convalescing.

Look for items in matched sets. Usually a couch will have had two comfortable chairs, a rocking chair, a couple of end tables, and a coffee table. Many sets had a dining table with six chairs to match as well. If you are not lucky enough to find all the items together, you can mix and match, but try to stay within the same decade. You will discover that 1950s furniture does not mix well with pieces from the 1920s.

PREVIOUS PAGES: An iron trellis overhead can help mark the setting for an outdoor dining room. In a dense garden setting, a beautiful bench can focus and soothe the eye. ABOVE: Hotels in the 1930s often commissioned metal garden furniture that would be durable and attractive even in harsh weather. RIGHT: Some furniture doesn't need cushions, making it truly carefree.

Old wooden furniture can also be fun to collect, but it might be harder to find items all in one piece. Cedar, redwood, and teak can withstand years of outdoor use, but not all old furniture was made from water-resistant wood. It may not have been designed to last more than a decade or two, so look out for rot.

Paint is the key to the longevity of old wooden garden furniture. If a piece was regularly painted each year or so and not left out all winter, it could survive a hundred years. Adirondack chairs are some of my favorite wooden pieces, and most were repainted year after year. They look as smashing in their fiftieth year as they did in their first.

Wooden park benches are wonderful, but look for the ones with iron arms and legs. If they are all wood, they will tend to fall apart much faster. If you find furniture with a couple of pieces of wood already replaced, beware. The bench has been rotting and may not hold out much longer.

If your garden space is small, you will not want your furniture to overpower it or take up too much space. But do not go too small. Garden furniture should be comfortable and practical. A teeny café table will not serve your guests or your dinner parties well. Glass-topped tables are a great solution for a tiny space: you can cover a large table base with glass because it takes up a lot less room visually.

AUCTIONS, FLEA MARKETS, AND ANTIQUE STORES

When my city friends come to my house in New Hampshire for the weekend, all they want to do is go to a country auction. I must admit, it is one of my favorite ways to spend a day. On-site auctions—outside, shaded by a big tent, overlooking some spectacular view, entertained by the music of the auctioneer's patter—are the very best.

Even after a decade of hunting and gathering, it still takes time—sometimes years!—to find that perfect piece. My shop, ABOVE, was always chock-full of gems that took some patience to uncover.

SAP BUCKETS

FROM NEW

HAMPSHIRE HOLD

EQUAL PARTS WATER

AND CHARM

The theater of the auction is enough for some of my friends. Others must bid, whether they really want something or not. This is the auctioneer's goal, to whip us all into such a frenzy of excitement that we forget what we are doing and spend more than we want. But, for the most part, auctions are still good places to find some great deals. Garden furniture is usually quite cheap at auctions that have a lot of good household furniture, since most people are there to furnish the inside of their homes, not the outside.

To find out where the auctions in your area are, look for auction listings in the classified sections of your local newspapers. Usually there is one paper in an area that has the best auction listings. Any antique dealer in your town will know which one it is. Not all will share the information, so you may have to ask a few. More and more auctions are advertising on the Internet, and some auctions are actually held on the Web. But I am an old-fashioned girl. I like the tent, the hot dogs, and the crowd when I am bidding.

When you go to an auction, set a budget for the whole day. Absolutely stick to it. Try to get to an auction early enough to look over the items on sale before the bidding starts. There is nothing worse than spending top dollar on an old iron urn that you later discover has a big crack in it. Some of the better auctioneers will mention the flaws in an item as it comes up—many will not. Sit in the front of the crowd. If you put most of the crowd behind you, you will not get distracted or too revved up by what

ABOVE and PREVIOUS PAGES: The charm and simplicity of old metal watering cans and sap buckets can turn any dark corner of a garden into a place of romance. Collections of pieces nestled and displayed together can make as much of a statement as a designer rosebush. And without the care! This bistro table from France, RIGHT, found its way to Maine, where I bought three of them in an auction. I wish there had been fifty!

other bidders are doing. Bid only on things you absolutely love. If you just like it, you will be sorry you bought it, I guarantee. Set a limit on each item you want to bid on before it comes up. Never raise your limit once you find yourself in a bidding war. This is tempting, but the item is probably worth only what you originally wanted to pay.

If, however, you find yourself at an auction where a few people are buying just about everything, rest assured that they are dealers. They plan to sell their pieces elsewhere for 20 percent to 100 percent more than they paid at the auction. With a quick calculation, you can use their bids to determine the value of an item. This is not to say that you should always try to outbid obvious dealers. They may be special collectors or taking their loot back to New York or Atlanta, where prices are much higher than in Kansas or Wyoming.

If you are lucky enough to want the first thing offered in an auction, go for it. It takes most people a few items to warm up, and the first item traditionally goes for a song. Be prepared to take home everything you have purchased that day. Some auctioneers will allow you to pick up large items the next day, but never assume this. Find out the requirements before you bid on that hollowed-out canoe that you thought would make a nice planter, only to realize it is fourteen feet long and will not fit on top of your car.

Flea markets can be real gold mines. I once bought twenty-five wooden sap buckets from a retired maple-sugar farmer in Vermont for twenty-five cents apiece. I had bought similar ones the year before for twelve dollars each at an auction.

Flea markets are held weekly all over the world. They can be an endless source of entertainment and cultural history. Before I travel anywhere, I find

RIGHT: My absolute favorite pastime is to go to New York City's huge outdoor flea market with my cousin Allison. Getting there early is the key to snagging the real prizes right as they come off the truck. LEFT: And it doesn't take long for chairs to find an old iron table and the perfect terrace setting to call "home."

out the location of the best flea markets are near my destination. The one just outside the Vatican in Rome is my personal favorite, but I have yet to hit the famous one at Clignancourt in Paris. Every Saturday and Sunday, spoiled New Yorkers are treated to one of the best flea markets in the world, come rain or come shine. There are enough accessories and garden furniture at the Twenty-sixth Street market to fill half the gardens in New York. Wherever you go, if you find garden items in the fall and winter, snatch them up and store them. They will be much more expensive in the spring. Besides, you will surely regret it if you have nothing to sit on that first warm day in April.

If you really want the gems of any flea market, get there early. If your local market is anything like those in San Francisco, New Orleans, and New York, dealers arrive as the trucks are unloading at dawn. The best things are snatched up before they hit the pavement. Often items move from booth to booth, increasing in price as they go. By the time you arrive at ten A.M. you will have to buy your prize for three times what it would have cost at five A.M. But no matter what you pay at a flea market, if it is going to your home, not to a store for reselling, you probably got a deal. The best thing about it is that you are recycling a bit of the past.

Antique stores are generally at the top of the old-furniture food chain. Usually the best pieces and the highest prices are found in antique stores. I buy plenty of things from stores. After years of designing gardens and buying

FLEA MARKETS ARE

antiques for them, I have learned which items will not be found easily elsewhere. The best things to buy in a shop are the most unique and fully intact pieces. A complete set of 1920s wrought-iron garden furniture with cushions may never show up at auction. Statuary and garden ornamentation is so hot now that finding it anywhere but in specialty antique stores is rare.

As old garden things become more popular, they become more expensive. If you cannot afford an entire garden of antiques, good reproductions can be found for a third of the price. If you can afford one authentic piece, highlight it. You may elevate your reproductions by close association.

Negotiating a good price is an old art. Don't haggle; the experience should be fun as well as respectful. Ask for the best price and walk away if you think it is too much. There will always be something else just around the corner.

Finally, family and friends are absolutely the best source of good old stuff. One man's trash is another man's treasure. Let people know you are in the market for old garden stuff, and you may not have to spend a dime. Be careful though, to accept only things you really do like. You will be stuck with them for a very long time if you have even the slightest sense of guilt.

HOW TO FIX IT

Just about any time you buy a piece of old furniture you will have to do something to fix it or shore it up. Before purchasing any old piece, know your limitations and tolerance for repair. Some things are easy to fix and other things are generally not worth the effort. Dealers seem to have a wide range of opinions on what is repairable and what is not. Unless the item is really cheap, I would

FULL OF GREAT OLD GARDEN GEMS

THE ORIGINAL PAINT AND RUST

ARE IRREPLACEABLE

wonder why the dealer did not fix the problem if it as easy as he or she claims!

Iron furniture can sometimes be repaired by welding, but when it rusts in crucial support areas, it is usually not worth it. If you find a chair broken at the bend in a key structural spot, walk away from it. Beware of furniture that has already been repaired, because it is likely weaker in an important area and could break again. Repaired furniture should be much cheaper than old furniture in perfect condition. Weigh the price differences against the length of time you can enjoy a piece before it breaks again. Sometimes it is worth buying something, knowing you have not spent much for a chair that may last only one season.

Look for rust in critical joints. If the rust is simply on surfaces where the paint has chipped, you may be able to get away with simple rust removal and a new paint job. If the bolts and joints are almost rusted through, do not buy it.

It is a bit more tricky to know if wooden furniture will last outdoors. As I've mentioned, the best woods for weathering harsh elements are teak, cedar, and redwood. Some painted wooden furniture can hold up for a hundred years. Look for signs of rot in tables that have been left outside. If a table has spent its life indoors, there is really no way of telling how it will withstand constant moisture. Most wooden tables and chairs do rot and warp outdoors. Painting wood with an outdoor finish will postpone the process but will not eliminate the possibility. I would not recommend putting a valuable wooden piece outdoors, but an inexpensive old pine table that you cover with a

PREVIOUS PAGES: An old mirror can reflect plenty of charm as well as the garden on the other side. The oldest iron gates predate soldering; they have an iron joint wrapped at every junction to keep them intact. LEFT and ABOVE: Newer iron pieces are simple, decorative, and functional with solder joints.

couple of coats of flat polyurethene each year could last a decade or so. Take all your garden furniture in for the winter if you have the space. There is no need to expose it unnecessarily.

The most common problem with old furniture is that it is not sturdy. I carry a little wrench and an all-in-one screwdriver when I go to an auction or a flea market. If a wobble cannot be fixed by a simple tightening of a few screws, let it go. Look underneath a coveted piece for added nails and screws. If it has been repaired in a shoddy way, I assume the repairs will not hold. There's nothing worse than serving a fresh garden salad on your new antique table and having it end up on your guest's lap. Keep looking; there is always another great table just around the corner.

Though I adore old chipped paint, I do think a good thing can be carried too far. It is best to remove any flakes that are falling off. I would not remove all the paint, just the flakes. Begin the removal with a little soft steel wool or a not too stiff wire brush. Gently remove the loose paint. Then, with very fine sandpaper, gently rub along the grain of the wood. With a damp cloth, wipe the paint dust off the surface. For most painted furniture this should be sufficient. Rub your hand over the piece to check for more flakes or any splinters. For a smooth, slightly waxy look, rub butcher's wax in a circular pattern over the entire piece. This will further clean the furniture while sealing it somewhat from water and dirt. Butcher's wax is a more porous natural finish than polyurethene. It will not alter the antique finish, nor will it completely protect the wood from heavy moisture.

ARCHITECTURAL ELEMENTS

Nothing accents a garden more than a wonderful sculpture or a fabulous fence. What a magnificent painting does for a living room, an old statue can do for a humble garden. Though there

ABOVE and RIGHT: Stone statuary, iron gates, urns, and wooden columns aged by weather need little enhancement and fit into any garden setting. FOLLOWING PAGES: A reproduction chandelier and two-hundred-year-old balustrades are right at home together, making my own garden a personal paradise.

are some terrific reproductions of architectural elements, try to find something affordable that has a bit of age to it. New statuary and new fences just never have the same great detail or patina.

There is a wide range of garden statuary available. Sotheby's auctions off $6,000 statues of cherubs, but a Rhode Island estate sale might take $100 for a similar piece. It has become harder to find great deals, but they are still out there if you know where to look. Any broken piece of statuary will go for much less than a piece in mint condition. I actually prefer the

ones with cracks and flaws. I think a piece shows more character if it is flawed. Plant some succulents or pansies in the crack of a great urn or statue and no one will be the wiser.

When visitors stroll through my gardens, they invariably stop and comment on the nonliving elements even more than on the flowers. I, too, find myself more drawn to the fountains and birdbaths at the Boboli Gardens in Florence than to the endless rows of cypress trees lining the entrance. In the winter a statue is most appreciated, elevating a barren landscape to almost mythical proportions. Something as simple as an old birdbath or a stone swan can focus a meditation on the changing season.

In choosing sculpture or architectural elements, look for pieces with classic lines. Cute ornaments will distract from the elegance and simplicity of any well-designed garden. A good rule of thumb is: the simpler the design, the longer it will remain in favor. The more curly and flowery a piece is, the sooner it will go out of fashion or turn from beautiful to ugly before your very eyes. Of course, all rules have their exceptions, and when it comes to buying architectural art, all choices are subjective. Buy what you love (not just like) and you will probably not go wrong. If you stop loving it, grow some vines around it, and it should become a favorite again.

FAVORITE FLEA MARKETS

Rose Bowl Flea Market
213.587.5100/213.588.4411
100 Rose Bowl Drive
Pasadena, California
Second Sunday of the month

**Santa Monica Outdoor Antique
and Collectible Market**
323.933.2511
Santa Monica Airport
Santa Monica, California
Fourth Sunday of the month

Georgetown Flea Market
202.223.0289
Wisconsin Ave. and S Street NW
Washington, D.C. 20037
Every Sunday

Scott Antique Market
614.569.4112
Atlanta Exposition Center
I-285 at Jonesboro Road
Atlanta, Georgia
Second weekend of the month

**Kane County Antique and
Flea Market**
630.377.2252
Kane County Fairgrounds
Randall Rd b/n Rtes. 38 and 64
St. Charles, Illinois

Bouckville Antiques Pavilion
315.893.7972
Route 20
Bouckville, New York
Every Sunday, May to October

**The Annex Antiques Fair and
Flea Market**
212.243.5342
Sixth Avenue and 26th Street
New York, New York
Every weekend

**Stormville Airport Antique Show
and Flea Market**
914.221.6561
Stormville Airport, Route 216
Stormville, New York
One weekend per month from
April to October

Metrolina Exposition Flea Market
704.596.4643
7100 Statesville Road
Charlotte, North Carolina
First Saturday of each month and
preceding Thursday and Friday and
following Sunday

Hartville Flea Market
Route 619
Hartville, Ohio
Every Monday and Thursday

Renninger Antiques and Collections
717.336.2177
Route 222
Adamstown, Pennsylvania
Every Sunday

Shupps Grove Antique Market
717.484.4115
1686 Dry Tavern Road
Denver, Pennsylvania
Saturdays and Sundays, April to
October

FAVORITE PLACES TO BUY FURNITURE AND CONTAINERS

Shabby Chic
800.876.3226/310.258.0660
6365 Arizona Circle
Los Angeles, CA 90045

Allan Davis at Y and Art
415.336.6002
2188¹/₂ Sutter Street
San Francisco, CA 94115

Zonal
415.563.2220
2139 Polk Street
San Francisco, CA 94109

Micheal Trapp
203.672.6098
7 River Road
West Cornwall, CT 06796

Trader's Way
970.249.3745
17656 Highway 550
Montrose, CO 81401

Pink Juntique
305.853.2620
98275 Overseas Highway
Key Largo, FL 33037

R. Wood
706.613.8525
348 Georgia Drive
Athens, GA 30605

The Pottery
706.335.3120
100 Pottery Road
Commerce, GA 30529

Assemblage
410.778.9747
PO Box 400
419 Broad Street
Crumpton, MD 21628

Antiques On Nine
207.967.0626
Route 9
75 Western Avenue
Kennebunk, ME 04043

Arundel Antiques
207.985.7965
PO Box E
Kennebunkport, ME 04046

Corey Daniels
207.646.5301
2208 Post Road
Wells, ME 04090

Country Mouse Antiques
207.646.7334
2077 Sanford Road
(5 miles north off Rt. 109)
Wells, ME 04090

Seaver McLellan
603.563.7144
Intersection Route 101 and 137
Dublin, NH 03444

Burlwood Antique Center
603.279.6387
Route 3 at Junction of Rt. 104
Meredith, NH 03253

Antiques of Moultonboro
603.476.8863
Old Route 109/26
Moultonboro, NH 02354

Gary Wallace Auctioneers
603.539.5276
1030 Route 16
Ossipee, NH 03864

The Ewings
603.569.3861
65 Federal Corner Road
Tuftonboro, NH 03816

1810 House Antiques
800.560.5349/603.569.8093
458 Centre Street
PO Box 1810
Wolfeboro, NH 03894

The Architectural Attic
603.569.8989
Clark Plaza/ Route 28
PO Box 1003
Wolfboro Falls, NH 03896

Potluck Studios
914.626.2300
23 Main Street
Accord, NY 12404

Hunters and Collectors
516.537.4233
Montauk Highway and Poxabogue
Bridgehampton, NY 11932

Ruby Beets
516.537.2802
1703 Montauk Highway
Bridgehampton, NY

Mulford Farm Antique Show and Sale
516.537.0333
Main Street and James Lane
East Hampton, NY

Ar Breizh
212.243.8683
37 Bedford Street
New York, NY 10014

Archetique Enterprises
212.563.8003
123 West 28th
New York, NY 10001

John Derian
212.677.3917
6 East Second Street
New York, NY 10003

The Lively Set
212.807.8417
33 Bedford Street
New York, NY 10014

Planter Resource
212.206.7687
106 West 28th Street
New York, NY 10001

Rhubarb Home
212.533.1817
26 Bond Street
New York, NY 10012

Rooms and Gardens
212.431.1297
290 Lafayette Street
New York, NY 10012

The Treasure Shop
914.247.0802
92 Partition Street
Saugerties, NY 12477

Valleyview
800.587.2535
7281 Warren Sharon Road
Brookefield, OH 44403

Chagrin Antiques
440.247.1080
516 East Washington Road
Chagrin Falls, OH 44022

Chagrin Valley Antiques
440.338.1800
15605 Chillicothe Road
Chagrin Falls, OH 44022

Antiques of Chester
440.729.3395
7976 Mayfield Road
Chesterland, OH 44072

Aunties Antique Mall
15567 Route 422
P.O. Box 746
Parkman, OH 44080

Farnsworth
330.296.8600
126 East Main Street
Ravena, OH 44266

I-76 Antique Mall
888.476.8976
Lyn Drive
Ravena, OH 44266

Adams Antiques
717.335.0001
2400 N. Reading Road
Denver, PA 17517

Grandma's Attic
717.733.7158
1862 West Main Street
Ephrata, PA 17522

Potting Shed
717.354.8484
148 East Farmersville Road
Ephrata, PA 17522

Leesburgh Station
724.748.3040
1753 Perry Highway (Route 19)
Valent, PA 16156

Eastern Shore Pottery
757.331.4341
26507 Lankford Highway
Cape Charles, VA 23310

Carvati's Inc.
804.232.4175
104 East 2nd Street
Richmond, VA 23224

FAVORITE PLACES TO BUY PLANTS

White Flower Farm
203.567.0801
Route 63
Litchfield, CT 06759

Pikes Family Nursery
404.633.6226
3935 Buford Highway
Atlanta, GA 30345

Eco-Gardens
404.294.6468
PO Box 1227
Decatur, GA 30031

Surrey Gardens
207.667.4493
PO Box 145
Surrey, ME 04684

Carvalho Greenhouses
914.266.3801
286 Hollow Road
Clinton Corners, NY 12514

Atlantic Nurseries (Wholesale Only)
516.586.6242
691 Deer Park Avenue
Dix Hills, NY 11746

Bissett Nursery (Wholesale Only)
516.493.1600 and 516.289.3500
470 Deer Park Avenue
Dix Hills, NY 11746

Otto Keil
516.692.7627
30 East Gate Drive
Huntington, NY 11743

Farmers Market
Union Square (at 16th Street)
New York, NY
Every Monday, Wednesday, Friday,
and Saturday

Shale Hill Farm and Herb Garden
914.246.6982
134 Hommerville Road
Saugerties, NY 12477

Auburn Point
440.543.7455
10089 East Washington Street
Auburn, OH 44023

Burton Floral
440.834.4135
13020 Kingsman Road
Burton, OH 44021

Art Form Nurseries
440.338.8100
156 Chillicothe Road
Chagrin Falls, OH 44022

Breezewood
440.543.2124
17600 Chillicothe Road
Chagrin Falls, OH 44023

Lowes Greenhouse
440.543.5123
16540 Chillicothe Road
Chagrin Falls, OH 44022

Bremack
440.729.7438
12265 Chillicothe Road
Chesterland, OH 44072

Sunnybrook Farm
440.729.7232
9448 Mayfield Road
Chesterland, OH 44072

Bluestone Perennials
800.952.5243
7211 Middle Ridge Road
Madison, OH 44057

Rock Bottom Farm (Jonathon Ford)
440.693.4126
7767 Parkman–Mesopotamia Road
Middlefield, OH 44062

Esben Shades
717.626.7007
546-A East Division Highway
Lititz, PA 17543

Ken's Greenhouse
717.768.3922
3552 West Newport Road
Ronks, PA 17572

Sterling Garden Center
803.252.7333
320 Senate Street
Columbia, SC 29201

INDEX